GW01388315

NINETY YEARS WITH

NINETY YEARS WITH DOGS

Dorothy M. Norris

Dorothy M. Norris

© Dorothy M. Norris, 2023

Published by Bramble Publications

A CIP catalogue record for this book is available from the British Library.

ISBN 978-0-9548253-1-7

Book layout and cover design by Clare Brayshaw

Cover image Illustration 96804137 © Celia Ascenso | Dreamstime.com

Prepared and printed by:

York Publishing Services Ltd
64 Hallfield Road
Layerthorpe
York YO31 7ZQ

Tel: 01904 431213

Website: www.yps-publishing.co.uk

*This book is in memory of my canine companions
and is dedicated to my three children, grandchildren
and great grandchildren and the dogs who have become
such important members of each family through the decades*

Contents

Preface

When looking back over many decades, there are different ways of remembering. Lots simply is forgotten or so buried under other details that it rarely resurfaces, if at all, unless triggered by something unexpectedly. Some memories even seem better avoided and consigned to the past while others are shared and reshared over time too. Retelling gives them a shape and form that includes some details and omits others. Following one strand of remembering the journey of life has its own appeal too: a way to relive and reflect that provides a focus and continuity through what, as the following pages reveal, has been a series of up and down episodes in different places and times.

The idea of writing something about my life with dogs has been around for a while. Dogs have been such constant companions over the years and brought much comfort, pleasure and at times, a profound sense of security. My dependence on dogs as friends, confidants and listeners is undeniable. They, and their need for care, have helped to steer me through difficult times and to give purpose to the day ahead. What better than to turn to my doggy memories when the COVID pandemic struck in 2020? Lockdown came eight weeks after my dog Leo died. I had already decided that I would not own another. I had to face the daily unfolding of an international horror story without a canine friend.

Lockdown imposed an unprecedented level of isolation even by my own standards of living alone in remote places. Unable to hug, to talk to people other than through windows, to go anywhere, I was connected to the outside world only via the phone, Skype and doorstep deliveries of groceries. Even letters through the post seemed to stop. The daily announcements from government ministers and medical experts brought the crisis into our homes relentlessly. Weeks turned into months. Masks distorted voices and, even worse for someone with poor eyesight, obscured faces. When socially distanced doorstep visits became possible, the inability to see or touch perpetuated lockdown ordeal. I dealt with the pandemic by taking my thoughts somewhere else. I found comfort as I wrote down my memories of living with dogs. Other details crept in too although it was never intended to be an autobiography. It is a celebration of canine companionship. I hope that others may find pleasure and enjoyment in their own dogs as I have done for so many years.

Dorothy M. Norris
West Yorkshire, January 2023

CHAPTER ONE

The importance of dogs

There have always been dogs in my life. Toby was the first, my father's dog, born a few years before I arrived on the scene in Victoria, British Columbia in Western Canada, June 1929. I do not remember Toby, but I am sure he sniffed at the new arrival, guarded the pram from dangers only he perceived, and later tolerated the small hands that grabbed his shaggy back.

My mother, sister and I returned to Great Britain as it was then known within a couple of years. I was still small, and golden from the Pacific sun and island air, a colour soon to disappear in our new home on the moorlands of Staffordshire. From an urban home in the expanding colonial settlement of Victoria, we had to adjust to the often bleak hilltop home we now shared with three generations of our English family. It was bewildering. We overlooked the Trent valley from our craggy perch, with the Potteries' great bottle ovens, coal mines and steel works in the distance. I could not see them with my myopic vision but this would not be detected for some years. There was a steep green slope below our small walled garden and it was not long before I lost my much loved wooden hoop among its rocky outcrops, crying bitterly as I had few toys.

The nearest buildings were a farm and outbuildings where I spent many daylight hours. Those were the days when children could safely roam or, at least, adults voiced fewer concerns. A farm was an ideal playground with straw, mud, chickens and ducks, half empty stone barns, and cowsheds still warm and pleasantly smelly from their overnight residents. Occasionally there was a blur of a scurrying rat, but I loved the rustle of mice wherever there was hay. Occasionally I saw the farmer's wife doing some late milking into a pail, electricity having not yet reached the outbuildings or, for that matter, the farm house. I loved to watch the great carthorse being led across the yard with its harness jingling and catching the early morning sun, but the most important reason to be there was to see my friend.

She was a rough haired collie called Molly although the farmer called her Moll. She had a long haired coat of black, brown and sandy colours. She often roamed freely but she also spent long hours tethered and lying in her kennel at the entrance to the cobble stone yard. With just her head visible she watched the comings and goings around the farm, her eyes and ears alert. When I approached she would rise to greet me, her lovely brush of a tail waving lazily to and fro before lying down again in the same place. I do not recall when I first joined her in her spacious shelter. Possibly a sudden gust of wind or rain made me take cover but she cannot have objected. I was small enough to fit into the dark interior behind her amidst the sacks and rags that were her bed, and it was warm and comforting. I once hid there after getting into trouble at home and caused a frantic search when I failed to return. It was a farm worker who finally suggested where I might be.

We were friends for years, even after my family moved to a more spacious home about a mile away. I visited Molly as often as I could for I missed the wildness and disorder of our rocky hilltop and the comfort of her presence. The thought never entered my mind that she was getting older until the sad day when I found Molly was no longer there. Her memory is still dear to me.

The storm clouds of war were gathering over Europe when we at last had a dog of our own. Lady was actually my aunt's dog. Auntie Billy, a nickname from the First World War when she had kept goats to supplement the family's food. She was my mother's sister. She was a teacher, and our new property had been designed to accommodate not only the family home, but a separate school building where she and her mother, also a teacher, could continue to operate a private school. There was also space for stables and outhouses for the goats and other animals she would soon acquire. As the family had always owned a dog in the past, I imagine a dog was part of the plan, together with poultry, ducks, Belgian hares and much later a calf and a pig, raised and renewed annually. The dog was almost the last to arrive. My aunt called her Lady.

Lady was not very old and had a sad history, as her mother had been found with her puppies out on the moors, terrified and half starving. She was a Welsh border collie, black and white with the usual plume of a tail, and the puppies were obviously pure bred. How they came to the area was a mystery, locally speculated upon but never resolved. I had badly wanted a dog of my own and was disappointed when my mother pointed out she belonged to my aunt and would live not with us but in the schoolhouse next door. My aunt, ever the diplomat in our extended family, solved the problem and said I could own Lady's tail which was nonsense, but it meant a lot to me at the time.

Lady actually lived in one of the stables but was later housed in the corner of the school's combined kitchen and cloakroom. That became her sanctuary, even after the room had been reinforced with sandbags at the outbreak of the Second World War and became The Wardens' Post, a key part of civil defence and advising local people about what to do in case of attack. Lady was always a nervous dog, but seemed to accept the regular invasion of her space by my uncle and other local men together with the addition of a stretcher hung on the school's cloakroom pegs, and a stirrup pump and protective clothing in case of a mustard gas attack. There were other items, too, but Lady probably took their presence for granted, as the children did as they walked or ran through the room numerous times a day.

Provided no one disturbed her in her corner Lady was content. My aunt said she was highly strung which did not mean much to me then, conjuring up visions of the strings on my grandmother's mandolin twanging as they broke. Poor Lady had certainly suffered traumas out on the moors but she matured into a quiet reliable companion. She was very anxious during thunderstorms, tending to panic if left alone, and we soon discovered that she disliked us singing. We were not very kind as we thought it funny when she howled in unison, not understandlng that it must have hurt her ears. I only realised this some years later when she showed no reaction to the deeper notes of an organ.

Lady had very acute hearing, picking up and noticeably stiffening at the far away sounds of air raid warnings long before the nearest one in the valley started wailing. The distant sounds of anti-aircraft guns in the evening was a signal for someone to shout "Where's Lady?" and while she was being located I would slip out into the darkness of the garden to watch the distant search lights sweeping the sky, ever hopeful of seeing an aircraft caught in the twin beams.

As a family we had watched sheep dog trials when on holiday in Wales, but my aunt never considered Lady as a working dog. Auntie Billy rented land at the end of our lane and took our three nanny goats and any half grown kids there every morning to graze. Each had a collar and they were tethered on long chains to enjoy a fresh patch of grass each day. Lady, my aunt's outdoor shadow, accompanied them, stopping now and again when she found something interesting, ignored by and accepting the animals she saw daily. One day, for reasons unknown, the leading goat decided to suddenly run on ahead. It shocked my aunt but she was surprised when Lady rushed after it, caught its collar and effectively stopped the other goats who were following. From then on Lady stayed with the small herd as they walked to and from their pasture, watching them intently. Goats are intelligent creatures and as far as I know, none of them ran off again.

Throughout the war years I had long periods of illness followed by weeks of convalescence. My grandmother had passed away some time previously so my mother and aunt were both now teaching in the school next door. Their brother was also out all day. He taught at a school in a small mining community some miles away, so I spent many hours alone. I had pet mice and rabbits, and there were always cats in and out of the house, but Lady was never allowed inside.

I desperately wanted a dog of my own but my mother was not an animally sort of person. She hated the presence of the goats and the hens clucking around her when she hung out the washing, and saw nothing funny when she was followed into the kitchen one day by a file of ducks.

When my mother started teaching we had a lady in to cook the school dinners. She owned a pedigree spaniel and a neighbour had a pedigree setter, both a lovely red bronze colour. By some accident there had been a litter of 'pedigree mistakes', and with the connivance of my uncle and aunt she determined to give me one of the puppies, a little black bitch, to keep me company. My mother's objections were over ruled, as they usually were. She was the youngest of the three siblings, and really I think she found the puppy irresistible although she would not have admitted it. I called the puppy RAF, the Royal Airforce being my favourite in the armed services, and I am sure the dog's presence helped me to get well both then and later during other prolonged absences from school in my early teens.

I had no knowledge then that the keeping of pets during the early years of the war was actively discouraged, but maybe the advice from the National Air Raid Precautions Animals Committee had not reached the Staffordshire moors. When this came to my attention recently I thought of our only local signpost which should have been removed in case of invasion. Someone had indeed tried, but having loosened it had found that the ornate knob above the three arms had rusted firmly into position. The village children found it made an excellent swing when walking past and it daily pointed a different way. I think it remained in place for some considerable time.

RAF

I cannot recall my earliest walks with RAF. Probably due to my ill-health she stayed with me in the house and later the garden before I was able to go out. The family were great walkers and as the village had only an hourly bus service to the nearest town we were accustomed to walking long distances in all directions. I had a detailed knowledge of the local countryside. The entire family had always gone out together to gather the seasonal fruits, blackberries, bilberries, elder and rowan berries and rose hips, and my mother and aunt made jams, jellies and pickles. It was one of my aunt's many hobbies and was a real asset during later food shortages. The school had extra rations but I remember only enormous tins of orange jelly which must have arrived from overseas on one of the Merchant Navy shipping convoys, a perilous voyage, but we children did not think of such things.

I knew the pathways and bridle tracks, short cuts and canal tow paths for miles around and was later able to do my own exploring with RAF on a lead and Lady walking beside me. The dogs had bonded from the start. Lady had never had puppies of her own, and possibly RAF saw her as a mother figure when she first arrived. They had very different personalities, Lady quietly mature while RAF had boundless energy and a frisky joy of life, but I do not think they ever had a difference of opinion. Each had their own well defined space and they made perfect companions. When the day promised fine weather our school-cook would prepare a picnic lunch for me so I could spend longer out in the fresh air, times that have left such happy memories.

All animal feed was rationed which may have had something to do with the demise of our free ranging chickens and ducks. I am sure they ended up in the oven, a timely and useful end as RAF gradually developed the skill of a poultry thief. I recall our village Bobby (police constable) who was the friend of most people for miles around, bringing RAF back one dark night, his belt being used as a lead, with a dead chicken in his other hand. There was a feather still dangling from RAF's nose. "You better put this in the pot tonight," he told whoever answered the door, "and keep the little bitch in if you can." RAF always looked so innocent, but one has to learn fast where canine crimes are concerned.

RAF had grown into a beautiful dog, larger than her mother and with many of the characteristics of her father. Sometimes the sun catching her glossy black hair showed a reddish tint but no one would have guessed the colour of her parents. Her tail had not been docked and streamed out gracefully behind her. Unlike Lady who was completely trustworthy, RAF's freedom had to be restricted unless we were well away from the village. Fortunately our garden abutted fields and moorland, and our nearest farmer knew her well. She and I were frequent visitors there and she was not interested in either cows or the huge carthorses although I am sure any poultry we met fled cackling to safety.

RAF and Lady

Both Lady and RAF were very friendly dogs and greatly appreciated by the children who came to our school. They called Lady the goat dog, but over the years RAF became known as the school dog, some of the older children taking her out for walks during their playtime. The dogs' friendly approach to all and sundry however got me into profound trouble on one occasion. Walking across the fields bordering our local golf course, the dogs exploring a little ahead, they came across a German P.O.W (prisoner of war) brewing tea on a small primus stove in a ditch close to where a bus load of his fellows were working. By the time I caught up man and dogs were getting along famously. I was greeted with an effusive gush of broken English and he stroked my hair. I was blonde and had long plaits so I expect I reminded him of home.

The dogs and I did not linger as a planned walk lay ahead. It seemed an exciting rather than troubling encounter, at the time, and something to recount when I got home but soon forgotten. Returning much later in the day by road I saw the men climbing into their transport back to camp and thinking of my earlier encounter I waved goodbye. There were strict rules about fraternizing with the enemy, not that it meant much to me at that stage in the war, but some villager reported my innocent action to the family. As a result I received the only scolding I ever had from my uncle, the fact that I had upset him far more important to me than his anger which was hard for me to understand.

One of my favourite walks was across the fields to the nearest village and our local church. RAF could run free and even the last short stretch by road was safe as apart from the hourly bus there were only farm vehicles and one could hear the horse's hooves from a quarter of a mile away. I loved the solitude and the peace of the little stonebuilt church where my grandfather had been curate (assistant vicar) many years before. In those days churches were never locked and if the door was locked to stop it blowing open in the wind, the key was always left on a ledge and easy to reach. The dogs would follow me in and up the aisle to where there was a pedal organ and they would settle at the foot of the chancel steps while I sat down for an enjoyable half hour at the instrument.

Looking back I am sure RAF probably sniffed around a bit before relaxing, but they were both tired from their walk.

I played by ear, never having been able to read music clearly due to myopia. It was a mixture of hymns, folk songs, bits of Gilbert and Sullivan and some of my uncle's sea shanties. He had been in the Royal Navy in the First World War. I imagined the grandfather I had never met standing in the pulpit listening to me with pleasure, which probably he would not have done really as he seems to have been a bit of a puritanical character. Every so often I told the dogs I would not be long. They were used to it and slept on peacefully, knowing the routine and enjoying the cool quiet building and the sun light which sometimes streamed through the stained glass windows, warming the mat where they lay.

The years rolled on, and I left school. In 1946, when I went to college in London my mother, as mothers do, accepted caring for RAF as her responsibility. This had probably happened long before but children take a lot for granted, particularly when they have pets needing care through times of poor health. The school children helped out and RAF accompanied them on many school excursions, loved by all. With so few privately owned cars, dogs often travelled long distances with their owners both by bus or rail. Lady and RAF had always been part of our family excursions, either to the seaside or perhaps the nearest lakes where rowing boats could be hired. Due to numbers, our family always hired two boats, and Lady went in one and RAF in the other. She loved water and went over the side frequently, hoping to catch a duck. She never succeeded and was slow to learn the reason for the irritation of the nearest family member when she was hauled back on board and shook herself.

Once established in London, my life seemed far removed from the country idyll of my childhood memories. The city was trying to rise from the ashes of war, a slow process of clearing rubble, temporary repair and rebuilding. Following my college year, my uncle took me on a walking tour in France, two fascinating weeks where we not only experienced the aftermath of the chaos and destruction of the European conflict, the despair, food shortages and poverty, but also encountered tales of courage and much friendliness from people we met. I felt the whole world was in transit, a new experience to the seeming stability of my teenage years. Looking back it was a perfect preparation for the subsequent difficult years of living in London, years of love and loss, becoming a mother, the first job, accommodation, friendships, despair and happiness.

I had little time to visit home and later with two small children to care for alone, my own mother had to visit me, accompanied by RAF. She had been to London several times before, travelling from the Midlands by steam train for many hours, but one visit nearly proved disastrous. While my mother waited for a taxi outside Euston station, with her suitcase and the dog on her lead beside her, a vehicle accidentally hit RAF. Whether she was too close to the kerb we never discovered but the first I knew about the accident was when my mother arrived at my garden flat in Hampstead, followed by the taxi driver carrying an apparently dying dog. They were both upset and I remember he refused to accept the fare. RAF was laid on a hurriedly procured blanket in the corner of the kitchen and we could only wait for the end.

But RAF was a survivor. She loved life too much to give up although it seemed she might have a fractured leg or pelvis. RAF remained immobile for my mother's entire stay, creating a lot of work as her appetite returned, and it was obvious that she could not be moved. Our landlord and landlady had accepted RAF's presence without any protest, although in 1950s London it was still commonplace to see accommodation advertised with the words 'No Irish, No blacks, No dogs'. Prejudices took many ugly forms as a mother of two young children of shared heritage, I knew only too well. I had been concerned that keeping RAF with me until she was better might jeopardise our tenancy but I need not have worried. The couple were in their late 50s, perhaps early 60s, childless and had seen much better days. They had gradually been forced to rent off each floor of their house and our garden flat was the last to go, while they lived in a small section of the ground floor. We shared the stairs with them and everyone in the building shared the hall and front door. They were a volatile couple but we saw little of them unless they had a quarrel. They were sympathetic about RAF and as none of the doors had locks I am certain one of them checked on her needs when we were out.

RAF loved companionship and attention and I was so relieved when her tail began to show no sign of injury. At different points in a long convalescence, she managed to get up on her feet, then she went out into our garden and then she accompanied us across the road to the walks on Primrose Hill. It must have been the length of the school term when my mother was again free to travel down to London again and take her home. After that, RAF was never able to scramble over walls, but what a welcome she received from the school children who would share her happy spirit and companionship for the remainder of her long life.

CHAPTER TWO

Dogs large and small

My aunt had bought a caravan which was towed to a different part of the coast ready for the next summer holiday. There different family members could indulge in their various interests, history, biology, zoology, geology and archaeology. Of course the dogs came too so my children could enjoy their company when digging in the sand and exploring rock pools. I believe a second caravan must have been hired when everyone was present. I can recall with nostalgia the cramped interior of my aunt's van during a spell of bad weather and the smell of damp dogs, the sea and drying clothes. Such times are long past and there came a day when first Lady and then RAF were no longer with us and life moved on.

Our lives in London, interesting but extremely challenging at times, always had a background desire of a return to the countryside, now a place just for holidays and escape. There was no room in our home for a dog and there were few if any in our neighbourhood. Our small garden flat in Primrose Hill was now just part of past memories.

By the later 1950s, our home was a London house of three floors with a small garden. We had an *au pair* to look after my third child while I worked all day and also a succession of cats. The latter were a necessity to keep the small and large London rodent population from taking over. I can still remember the rats at some of the underground stations running in and out of the tunnels while people waited for the next train. There were dogs in the outer suburbs but in the West End one was more likely to see a miniature poodle with a diamante collar and coat tinted to match their owner's hair, a lavender shade being then popular. The type of dog I loved and yearned for often was completely absent. I cannot recall seeing even a guide dog in those days.

Many events and changes would occur before once again bad health intervened in the course of my life and we would again find ourselves back in the countryside. Illness, however debilitating, is a useful time to take stock, to plan a new course in life and in my case to shape a new career. My eldest children were in their final years at boarding school, the youngest attending the family's still surviving private school. On her seventh birthday she was given a dog.

Wilhelmina, soon to be shortened to Willie, was a little Welsh Corgi. I imagine she came from the pet shop in the nearest town, where as a child I used to sell my surplus pet mice for sixpence each. No one had heard of puppy farming in those days. Willie was a sturdy little dog, a plump puppy but with the promise of a long body. She had the very short legs so characteristic of her breed, and had short reddish brown hair with a few white patches, and a stubby tail, a complete contrast to past family dogs. Her love of life and the way her emotions were reflected in the waggle of her little tail won everybody's heart, and she was quick to learn what behaviours were not acceptable. As a puppy she was very possessive of things she treasured. Someone once gave her a knuckle bone almost as big as herself. It was meant as a joke as her little teeth could not have gripped any part of it but she guarded this treasure in a fearsome way and it took some subterfuge to eventually get rid of it. When she remembered she searched for it again and again. Of course, Willie was not my dog, but the responsibility was mine and as with all family pets one becomes increasingly fond of them, looking after their welfare as their owners grow and finally move on.

In the mid 1960s, I bought a very old and abandoned building. It had been a public house and still had the licence for alcoholic drinks attached to the freehold which I dispensed with at the time of purchase. I was unaware that the building was in the process of being eaten away by woodworm and I think the whole place was held together by the huge millstone grit blocks with which it had been constructed. In retrospect it was a better choice than an old farm empty and for sale that I had discovered some months previously. The place was nearer my first English home but there were legal problems and the location would have been much too remote for daily travel. With hindsight, both options were completely eccentric but at least, the house we bought was more affordable with the help of a mortgage, not easy to arrange in those days as a single woman. Fully recovered from my last illness, I had found a temporary job, and was anticipating being accepted as a mature student at the local teacher training college. The old pub, although remote, was fortunately on an hourly bus route and not too far from my new job and the college.

We had a large enclosed cobbled yard at one side where horse drawn wagons had once pulled in to offload the barrels of beer. It was an ideal place for Willie's favourite game.

She had a large ball and when it was kicked towards her she was adept at stopping its progress and heading it back to the sender. Her energy was inexhaustible and she would go on enjoying the activity until her playmate just gave up. She would then nose the ball around a few times before wandering off to find something else to do.

Jeremy and Willie

We had discovered while on holiday in the Brecon Beacons another activity Willie enjoyed. It was an ideal area for flying kites and when she saw our simple handmade one trembling on the ground prior to the initial run and launch Willie began to get excited, barking non-stop, then chasing excitedly after the runner until the wind carried the kite skywards. Her barking became almost hysterical as it soared upwards until she could do no more than stand quivering with eagerness waiting for whatever would happen next.

Her reaction was always the same and I hoped she could experience this doggy thrill when we returned home. The kite did not have a long life and no one made another due to a mixture of other interests and the position of our house. This part of the Staffordshire/Cheshire border was at an altitude of 1000 feet where we enjoyed some days with no wind at all and sometimes gales so fierce that it was hard to stand upright away from the shelter of the nearest wall, not ideal conditions for flying kites.

We had twelve bantams and their fierce 'husband', a feisty cockerel who strutted around the yard and the large outhouse where they all roosted. A series of vaulted cellars led off this building but Willie never ventured into this area, intimidated by the ferocious bird, although when he was no longer around she still kept out of the building and away from the more gentle hens. We found them delightful. Occasionally they would fly on to one's arm when they were fed, and they provided us with many small eggs. Willie kept to the perimeter wall, yapping excitedly if anyone walked past even though she could not see them, and wagged her little tail with satisfaction after they had gone past, pleased that she was guarding her territory so well.

Willie seemed to be attracted to large dogs and some found her of great interest, too. We learnt this inadvertently and partly because I was too busy to notice the signs. The yard wall was at least two metres high and the entrance gates equally solid and impregnable, but at certain times dogs can surmount the seemingly impossible. One lusty Heinz variety managed to gain access, possibly because a farm vehicle had been parked in the lane close to the wall offering a step up and he just came over the top. We had to force the heavy gates open amidst the weeds to get him out again, but that dog became the father of Willie's first litter of puppies, not welcomed by me but soon loved and sadly missed when we found new homes for them. It is always a difficult but necessary task to part with young animals. Unfortunately Willie seemed to find an even larger dog next time and for a few years I had to deal with the same pattern. She had no problems giving birth and was an excellent little mother, but her next litter of three adorable puppies put her at great risk. Before I found homes for them their legs were almost the same length as their mother's height and the vet said they must be the last for Willie's sake. That final birthing had not been an easy one so I welcomed the vet's help and advice.

Meanwhile my eldest daughter, Claudia Ruth and her future husband had brought home a beautiful dog, offered to them as a Great Dane.[1] She was young, very aristocratic in her bearing and a lovely silver blue in colour. We all admired her and Willie seemed quite happy at the temporary companionship, but her presence brought a slow sad end to our family of bantams. Zarka would however pave the way for a new permanent addition to the family. Her presence was of great interest to some friends in the neighbourhood. Not long after her arrival they heard of a couple of Harlequin Danes that had been left in kennels and had been abandoned by their owner. The kennel proprietor had said they could no longer afford to feed them and that they would have to be put down. Our neighbours decided to go and have a look at the dogs and my son, Jeremy and younger daughter, Heather, accompanied them. The result was inevitable. They

---

[1] Always known in the family as a Great Dane, subsequent research has suggested that Zarka may have been a Weimaraner.

returned to the village with both dogs, the stronger of the two being kept by the neighbours and the other brought back to me, knowing that I was unlikely to refuse to take in such a dejected looking young animal.

Zarka

It was almost dark when they returned, and the preliminary discussion about the dog's future were still in progress when someone opened the front door and the dog fled out into the night. He must have been terrified after the long car journey and the sudden separation from his sibling. The search that followed was long and exhausting and I think we nearly gave up as it seemed a hopeless task in an area of rugged countryside, fields, dry stone walls and the occasional farm. It was this farm that ended our growing despair as the dog had taken refuge in the nearest open building, a shed where hay was stored. The farmer who supplied our daily milk found and shut him in before calling out that the dog was found. So we got him home again, safe on a lead, and settled down over a pot of tea to finish our former discussion on his future. This did not take long! He stayed and we called him Sebastian.

Sebastian

Sebastian was a pathetic picture, immature, very thin, and extremely nervous. His mainly black coat with small areas of white lacked any lustre and he showed nothing of the handsome dog he would become. He needed a lot of care and, after a visit to the nearest vet, my son and I were able to give him the daily injections that had been recommended. Regular meals, exercise and love soon transformed him from a quivering wreck into a confident and handsome companion who was both gentle and affectionate. Sadly his brother seemed to have inherited a vicious streak. I am not sure what happened to him but we were indeed fortunate in being offered the second choice!

For some months we enjoyed the mixed pleasure and problems of three dogs, two somewhat outsize and the other rather small. They got along with each other from the start, possibly because Willie seemed drawn to the larger members of her species, and Sebastian was originally too feeble to provide any threat or jealousy to either bitch. I think certain members of my family began as the weeks went by to dream of Zarka and Sebastian eventually having puppies but this would never happen.

Zarka was still at a destructive age while she was with us and apart from chewing holes in a pair of trousers managed to tear up a copy of Tolstoy's *War and Peace* one evening when she had been left shut in a bedroom. I do not recall that Sebastian ever destroyed anything, but he had to be watched during the preparation of meals. For dogs of his height it was too great a temptation to walk past a table spread for dinner when plates were conveniently level with his nose. Cooked or uncooked, a chop can disappear in a second. After a few mishaps, we all learned as rapidly as the dog, but I never trusted Sebastian completely when the table was set for a meal.

Another lesson we quickly learnt with Sebastian was that it was far wiser to walk a long distance than travel by bus. Willie was used to bus travel. We needed to use three different buses to reach my childhood home and when my dear uncle passed away my mother and aunt lived there alone. Our local double decker from the nearest town ended the journey just above our house where it reversed and came back to halt at our front door. It then manoeuvred slowly down a steep winding lane before the terrain became easier. Dogs had to be taken to the top deck and preferably to the back, an easy ascent for a long legged animal but harder for Willie. There was seldom any hurry as the driver took a short break, and I have seen the student members of my family on several occasions rise from their unfinished breakfast, mug in hand, to rush through the front door to board the bus. I always hoped the mugs would return in their bags at the end of the day.

Willie usually rode on the seat so she could see through the window while Sebastian would have to stand on the floor. On this particular occasion as the bus started moving, the floor slowly tilted and we moved out onto the steep hill, we saw to our horror a little rivulet of liquid move quietly down the centre of the gangway. Sebastian, coming straight from the house with no time for other matters, had 'leaked'! I can feel our embarrassment still. I have since experienced similar situations with a large dog on the car deck of a ferry, but the violation of the relatively clean floor of our local bus was highly embarrassing. We watched almost mesmerised as the flow advanced and retreated with the level of the floor during the next half hour, praying no other passenger would mount the stairs, and when we got to our destination alighting guiltily like a bunch of criminals, glad that the driver had left his seat. I think our guilt persisted whenever we used the bus for some time afterwards but it was never mentioned by the driver. Perhaps only the cleaner was ever aware of Sebastian's crime?

The next time my daughter, Heather, Willie, Sebastian and I undertook the same journey we left early in the day with a picnic lunch and an Ordnance Survey map. My mother was away and my aunt was alone so we wanted to check that she was all right. It was a beautiful summer's day, one where we could have lingered dreamily by the stream where we ate our lunch if there had been more time. Willie played and explored while Sebastian after a cursory view of our surroundings, lay down until we were ready to move again. The walk was a bit of a challenge, cross country and partly new terrain but we finally reached our destination much to my aunt's pleasure. The time together passed too quickly and leaving later than planned I risked making the journey home by bus. Fortunately the dogs were tired after their long and exciting day, and slept soundly all the way home. Bus travel with them was undertaken only when absolutely necessary for some years until I was able to have a car of my own.

CHAPTER THREE

Dogs at school and in other places

Time for thinking about another move had arrived. I had finished my teacher training and probationary year, my eldest child Claudia Ruth was married, my son, Jeremy busy shaping his own path through life elsewhere, and my youngest attending my old grammar school. The rugged upland weather conditions and very inadequate heating of our eighteenth century home was affecting my health but unlike previous moves it was not the prime motivation for my decision. Unexpectedly we received a rather advantageous financial offer for the building which I accepted. With no job or particular area in mind where I and my younger daughter, Heather, and the dogs could start life afresh, family discussions settled on a move to the Hampshire/Dorset area, conveniently close at that time to where my eldest was living. I knew little about these counties but the milder climate and proximity of the sea were attractive. I arranged to stay with Sebastian in the home of some of my elder daughter's friends while I found a job, a house and a new school for Heather. She and Willie would stay with my mother and aunt and continue at secondary school until I had accomplished these tasks.

Dogs are amazingly accommodating, adjusting easily to new situations provided food and shelter and the close proximity of the person they have bonded with are assured. Sebastian and I were now sharing a very small room in a semi-detached house with a young couple and their two small children who were well under school age. We were made to feel very welcome and the pittance I contributed was of help to the family budget. Nevertheless however well behaved Sebastian was, and he was very obedient, I could not leave him alone without my supervision. As a result we spent much of each day away from the house. I think looking back it must have been a period of very dry weather as we explored further and further afield looking for houses for sale. One of my most urgent tasks also was to visit the local authority education offices where I had already given them my details but there were no vacancies. It was getting towards the end of the school holidays and I was told to call back after the start of the new term, not that I was given any hope of a job.

At that stage finding a home was my first priority and I followed up every place within my price range, accompanied by Sebastian, at the same time getting to know the area and what it had to offer. He received a lot of attention and helped to smooth the way through problems that arose from time to time. The education office got very used to his presence as my visits gradually turned into daily ones, and estate office staff were more likely to greet him first when we walked through the door. It was not long before I found what I wanted but the process of buying would not be so simple. In 1970, it was very difficult for a woman to obtain a mortgage, however small, despite having been sole owner of two previous properties.

I had to get a letter from my family's bank manager, over two hundred miles away, to guarantee the payment before the deal was settled. It was humiliating! My daily visits to the education office were at last successful, too. It was a case of being in the right place at the right time. A head teacher had fallen ill. Could I act as her deputy immediately? I could and did!

Meanwhile, the house I had found was empty, the owner having passed away many months previously and legal issues were being finalised just when I came on the scene. I was able to move in as soon as the sale went through. Heather was accepted by a local grammar school and Willie and Sebastian could be together again. We were delighted to be reunited. What the dogs thought of it all was fleeting if they thought at all. They met as if they had only been apart for hours, not months. Willie's rear end wagged in pleasure and Sebastian checked her out from nose to tail with satisfaction on seeing her. They inspected their new home in their own way as thoroughly as we did, and gave the garden even more attention, tiddling and sniffing in every corner to establish the immediate past, present and any future possibilities.

Our new home was a typical 1930s semi-detached with two average sized rooms downstairs, kitchen, pantry, and spacious enclosed back porch. An exceptionally narrow hall and steep staircase led to three bedrooms and a bathroom. We had to adjust after all the space, albeit damp and shabby, that we had enjoyed in the north. When our possessions came out of store and were delivered, all went well until the final item was manipulated through the front door. It was a heavy unwieldy nineteenth century piano and it got stuck. The more the removal men heaved the more apparently permanently fixed it became and it was a relief when they gave up, completely defeated. The dogs could only go in and out through the back door and side entrance, and we could only go upstairs by crawling along the lid of the keyboard and top. It took considerable time and ingenuity the following day for the obstruction to be resolved and the instrument safely placed in our new back room, much to our relief and that of the removal firm.

Willie now became the self-appointed guardian of our small house. I imagine it was easier for her to guard than her previous home. Whenever anyone came to the front door she got there first, Sebastian following with his measured stride. When the door was opened Willie would often stand between his legs, barking quite ferociously although she never moved over the doorstep, a relief as the paved entrance, designed for a parked car, had no gate. It would be some time before I passed a driving test and was able to park my old Morris Traveller close to the doorstep.

Exercising the dogs at this time had to fit around the school routine. Sebastian and I knew the immediate area well from house hunting and job searching days. From my initial temporary teaching post, I moved on to a permanent position in a progressive primary and middle school with a visionary head teacher. His energy and personality inspired loyalty from his staff, including volunteering some of our free time. My younger daughter was also occupied in adjusting to life at a new school where the ethos was very different to where she had been previously. As both of us were away from the house for long hours five days a week, I think Sebastian and Willie must have spent much time alone in the house and garden. There was a long straight path on both sides with a privet hedge dividing us from the next house and a *Weigela* hedge between us and our next door semi. Willie often chased her large ball down the *Weigela* path and although the hedge was very attractive, particularly when covered with blossom, poor Willie became the object of irate tirades from our elderly neighbour when her toy rolled against the sturdy shrubs. The ball did no harm but we learnt to avoid such games when the irascible old man was outside. There was a rockery with a few shrubs separating our garden and back porch. It made a useful barrier to our side entrance and the road, so the dogs had a safe area to relax when it was sunny and do the things all dogs do in their daily enjoyment of life.

A scenic view point was only a short walk away from the house. It was a grassy area with wooded slopes overlooking the rapidly expanding sprawl of Poole in Dorset. The dogs could run free there, safe from traffic, and apart from the occasional coach of visitors during the summer we met few people. The ones we did meet were always ready to talk. Dogs of Sebastian's size attracted immediate attention, even if it was just the much repeated remark, 'Why don't you put a saddle on him?' Willie liked to explore, but Sebastian's exercise was more a sudden burst of speed and an equally quick return to stand at one's side apparently enjoying the view. There was one activity he soon discovered when we sat down on the one public bench. He came rushing back after some exploratory excursion and instead of slowing down shocked us by clearing the bench in one great bound, narrowly missing our heads. After that his pleasure in jumping whenever we reached the view point became such a feature of the walk that my first thought when approaching was to check if anyone was sitting there before I unclipped his lead. I think he had just accomplished one of his leaps when a coach of tourists drew up behind us and within minutes several delighted Chinese visitors were taking photographs of him. Fortunately our walks and tourists did not coincide very often, but it was amusing at the time.

One incident I did not find amusing was some of the exaggerated accounts I heard for a short time after we returned from a brief holiday. I had left the dogs in the care of Claudia Ruth and a teenage half brother. She had brought Zarka with her and the two Great Danes had been delighted to see each other again before we left. Our walks had sometimes coincided with two fashionably dressed ladies and their Salukis walking in the same direction as ourselves though on the opposite side of the road. The Salukis were always beautifully groomed and looked extremely elegant, aristocratic and well behaved. Their owners never acknowledged our presence even when the road was empty of traffic: I felt, rightly or wrongly, that they rather despised our practical dogwalking clothing and the excited corgi tugging ahead on her lead. It seemed as if the distinctive size, colouring and combination of our animals was not worth noticing compared with their own beautiful dogs, and the same sense of superiority extended to the people holding the leads too.

Unfortunately during our absence, Zarka and Sebastian found the front door had not been properly closed and slipped out, Zarka following Sebastian on his customary route. Upon seeing the Salukis what happened next was inevitable. They crossed the road and the Salukis took off, no doubt their alarmed owners dropping their leads.

The four large dogs chased down the steep hill which was very familiar to Sebastian from our once daily visits to the education office and it was on the Salukis' regular route to the nearest park. It is easy to imagine the havoc they caused as the large area of parkland was a haven for both land and sea birds and was regularly grazed by numerous Canada geese. There were also some rarer birds such as black swans on the lake. People did not have mobile phones in the 1970s so the dogs had a wonderful spell of freedom, chasing each other, scattering the wild life, and no doubt being far from silent before they were finally rounded up. I heard that the police had used nets in the end before they could be captured and restored to their homes but we heard so much nonsense on our return that we probably never heard the full truth about the incident.

My headmaster never ceased in his schemes to enhance the lives of his pupils. He called for the participation of his staff and the children's co-operation and actively encouraged any help that families could offer in fund raising or even building work. We had numerous jumble sales, fairs and other outdoor activities and shared his delight in what we jointly achieved. My daughter, Heather, who participated in many of these school activities thought of how we might use Sebastian's popularity to raise money at these events. She ran a competition where people had to guess his length from the tip of his nose to the end of his tail. They paid to take part and names and addresses and estimated lengths were carefully recorded, the winner to be notified and rewarded in due course. Many people had a go, few getting anywhere near the actual figure. They had never seen him standing with his front paws on our shoulders which might have given them some idea, but appreciated that he stood so patiently and was safe to be touched by their toddlers and pre-school children. The whole idea was a great success and the person with the nearest guess won a small prize without our revealing the actual figure, so we could use Sebastian as a fund raiser at future events.

Heather, Sebastian and Zarka

During my time as a member of this very happy and successful school community, the staff were aware that a new school had been planned and was being built in the area. Some of us went to view the building prior to completion. Its provision still reflected now discredited tendencies to label and separate young children into different schools on the basis of being 'uneducable', 'sub-normal' and 'malajusted'. The school was designed to bring together all these supposedly ESN (educationally subnormal children) rather than teach them in mainstream schools. Upon completion the local authorities invited teachers to volunteer for positions at the new school. I had a deep interest in children with special needs and many concerns about the labelling that often channelled children permanently away from mainstream classrooms and created great stigma. Although I was very happy where I was teaching, I decided to apply. I was accepted, a seemingly small move at the time, but one that would ultimately affect my future.

Very early on I realised that with a few exceptions, many of the children should have been retained in ordinary schools, just receiving extra support, instead of such an emphasis on their differences. As my new head teacher followed the latter school of thought, only his desire to make a success of his new school, and my own desire to do as much as possible for each child in my care, made the position tolerable. I soon realised that the new school was based on a principle of separation and a vision of segregation that was far from my own beliefs. I also found that Sebastian and Willie would not be welcomed at my new school. Sebastian, however, was to play an important part in my work during the years that followed.

We had many troubled children and their poor attendance, despite the provision of transport, was of great concern. We were instructed to make home visits and, aware of some of the backgrounds, it was a daunting prospect without guidance and support. I had several children from Travellers' families who had been resettled by the local authorities and put into council houses much against their will. One of my frequent absentees was a delightful and intelligent boy whose father had a known violent history.

The only way I could check comfortably on the missing pupil was to take Sebastian with me, his size offering me a sense of security as I ventured into the unfamiliar territory of home-visits. Strangers did not know how gentle he was, and Sebastian had always placed himself in front of me when confronted with anything unusual. On this occasion I was uncertain of what to expect and, upon opening the door, the father's expression did not inspire confidence. Sebastian's presence enabled me to make my enquiries and I learnt his son and other younger children were back in a camp on the nearby heathland. I knew the likely location, from previous walks, so thanking him as the door was violently shut, we set off again.

I think my approach had been seen from a distance. The only people visible were three women who I guessed were elderly but brimmed hats shielded their faces. They were sitting around an open fire with a large pot containing what I imagined was a meat and vegetable stew which one of them stirred from time to time. They were talking as Sebastian and I approached but one of them asked me what I wanted. She seemed to be the spokeswoman for the group so I apologised for my intrusion and explained that I was looking for a missing pupil. Sebastian stood beside me but the Travellers did not refer to him. I felt that we were all observing each other and listening very carefully.

I explained that the child's frequent non-attendance at school was spoiling his chances and said quite truthfully that he was the brightest in my class. He had no reading and writing skills when I first met him and was making excellent progress and was a joy to teach. The women murmured in appreciation and I gathered they were his aunts but I could not follow what she said about his whereabouts or that of his mother. I was assured he would attend more regularly and left feeling that good will had been established. I was pleasantly surprised some weeks later when the boy asked me to revisit his home which I duly did the following Saturday with Sebastian. Apparently some official looking letter had arrived which his father requested that I should open and read to him, his son having assured him I was 'orl righ(t)'. In fact I was able to help him in this way on several future occasions, assuring him that his son was well on the way to being able to read and would soon be able to help.

If only all such school visits could have had such a successful outcome. I was increasingly glad to have the presence of my large four legged companion when carrying out such visits until our sympathetic deputy head advised that if we felt threatened or uncertain about any visit we must use our own discretion.

CHAPTER FOUR

New opportunities and travels by car

When eventually I passed my driving test, the possession of a second hand Morris Traveller opened up a new world for us. Taking dogs for daily walks is an excellent way of learning one's immediate neighbourhood but we now enjoyed much longer walks at weekends and other outings. Heather went sailing on many Saturday mornings and when she was due to return, the dogs and I would walk down to the harbour jetty and await the boat's arrival so that she would have company on the long uphill route home. We enjoyed the park also, Sebastian and Willie safely on their leads, not only because of Saluki memories, but because it deterred the Canada geese from approaching too close. Their threatening behaviour frequently intimidated my daughter.

Petrol costs maintained old habits of long outings on foot. Another walk we appreciated was along the shore at Sandbanks where the dogs could run free and we could enjoy a picnic and do some beach combing on the exposed pebbles and muddy flats of Poole Harbour. On one occasion we got cut off by the incoming tide. We had to climb over the fence of one of the mansion-like dwellings along the shore line hoping no one would see us trespassing as we crept up the garden path back towards the road. Now sometimes known as Millionaire's Row due to the increase in property values, I do not recall ever seeing anyone in those large, windswept and sometimes neglected gardens. We usually had the shore to ourselves.

I was not a confident driver but there was much less traffic in the 1970s and we now had the whole of Dorset and Hampshire within reach. Following new legislation, I had a dog guard fitted to the Morris Traveller leaving ample space for Sebastian and Willie to stand or relax when on the move. We used to spend hours away from home with food and thermos flasks and water for the dogs. The only hazard we encountered that I recall was a group of skinheads on motor bikes but they had other things on their minds and let us go on our way. On one drive to the chalk downs, an exceptionally beautiful area, we encountered for the first time the lovely large blue butterfly not realising how rare such sightings were. Only a few years later it was extinct in the wild but I believe at the time of writing it has been successfully reintroduced in certain areas. There were many delightful little blue butterflies, too, also new to us, as we were more familiar with the butterflies that thrived on the vegetation and geology of further north.

Life was exciting, too, discovering the prehistoric barrows and tumuli dotted across the area, and visiting hillforts like Maiden Castle paved the way to other interests. Needless to say, Sebastian and Willie had equally interesting canine encounters before we all returned happily exhausted to the car. Strangely I have no memories of muddy, wet dogs or smelly journeys home, but perhaps I have forgotten the wet days!

The highlights of these Dorset excursions were our trips to Kimmeridge Bay, and the famed Jurassic coast notable for its fossils and the discovery in 1811 by Mary Anning of the skeleton of an ichthyosaurus. It must be every visitor's secret dream to make some similar fantastic discovery but, having had a lifetime interest in geology, the whole area had a particular fascination for me. I knew of the fragility of the Blue Lias cliffs before our first visit. The grey clay was prone to landslip, sometimes revealing spectacular discoveries like that of Mary Anning, but extremely dangerous, and I had to keep a close watch on Sebastian. Willie stayed with us as we searched for smaller fossils lying amidst the debris after a storm or high water, but Sebastian could cover quite a long distance in a very short time, leaping from one large boulder to the next with the joy of life and freedom. Fortunately he would return at equal speed when called. The incoming tide was always much in my thoughts, as no one could climb to safety on the slippery unstable cliffs, and it is easy to walk much further than planned when searching for a spiral ammonite or the cylindrical belemnites we hoped to find. There was one enormous ammonite, the largest I had then seen, partly eroded from the rocky shore. Willie and I could stand together on the huge fossil with room to spare. How I wish now that such moments could have been recorded on film, but we seldom then thought of such things, relying most of the time on memory or diary notes to recall highlights of each outing.

Dogs react to the sea in different ways, as varied as those of humans. Sebastian preferred not to get his feet wet though it happened on occasion when he got too close when chasing along the shore. Willie was more interested in rock pools although I do not think she could see more than the sun sparkling on the ripples caused by our hands. She enjoyed what we might later put on the sand beside her, particularly crabs. Their sideways movement was very exciting although she enjoyed even more the presence of gulls. She loved frightening them off their temporary perch on a boulder and barked excitedly as they took to the air. She was a very happy little dog.

From time to time my son, Jeremy, and his young family were able to share our enjoyment of the Jurassic coast, although they lived at some distance, but my eldest and her family, including Zarka, had left the area. Before their move we had been introduced to a kennel facility for Great Danes. It was owned by a delightful family where the mother had known the Dorset author, Thomas Hardy, and they possessed about six of their own huge golden brown Danes who shared the house with them and dwarfed both Zarka and Sebastian in size. I referred earlier to the initial hope that Zarka and Sebastian might have puppies but they had shown no interest, and it was arranged that Zarka should be mated to a suitable pedigree dog at these kennels. This failed in its purpose but it did introduce me to a suitable place to kennel our dogs when my younger daughter and I went away. They were willing to take Willie because she and Sebastian could share the same space, and over the next few years I felt very happy leaving them there, despite the long drive which did a lot to build my confidence on busier roads than the ones I used daily. Zarka never had puppies and sadly was not destined for a long life, but she left some very warm memories. Her name lives on in Spain.

At this period of our lives it became apparent that my mother and her now invalid sister needed to move nearer to younger family members and they expressed a desire to join us in Dorset. With this in mind I put our house on the market and we began to search for a larger property. We found what we thought was ideal, a pleasant home converted into two apartments with a lovely neglected garden which we could all enjoy. It was a little nearer the sea and in a far more congenial area than our present home and was standing empty. It has always surprised me how many properties are left uninhabited for months or even years through a variety of often strange reasons. My younger daughter and I liked it on sight. The property was within my price range, conveniently situated for both our schools, and only needed the sale of our present home so that I could finalise the deal. We were so confident about our future ownership that the estate agent entrusted us with the keys so that we could visit when we wished.

One Sunday, we and the dogs drove down to spend a happy couple of hours looking around, full of plans about what would go where. As usual I put the keys on the mantelpiece in the front room where the dogs usually settled down after their cursory inspection that all was the same as on our previous visit. Then we went out into the garden leaving the front door open as we had done on several previous visits. Empty houses tend to get musty. We knew the property was secure and the gates shut so Willie and Sebastian were safe from what little traffic there was on the quiet road. Suddenly the front door slammed shut, the dogs started barking and we were locked outside. We tried the front door, then the side and the back door, hoping desperately that one of them could have been left insecure, feeling more panicky by the moment. Meanwhile the dogs, quite accustomed to being left on their own at home for long periods, sensed that they were shut in and raised the volume of their voices to a degree that I thought would attract half the neighbourhood. It did not, proof that our assessment of a very quiet road was correct, but at the time I wished it otherwise.

Wondering what to do we went out into the road and were staring up at the building when a man on a bicycle came slowly towards us. He was an off duty policeman on the way home for lunch. He halted immediately, listened to our sorry tale and gave us confidence that things were not as bad as they seemed. I have never forgotten his cheerful comment, "One can get into most houses if one's desperate enough." Propping his bike against the wall he went into the garden to scrutinise the front windows. "Ha! As I thought," he said, and getting something out of his pocket he levered up one of the small window frames then common at the top of large bow windows. Turning to Heather, he suggested that if he lifted her up she was slim enough to reach through, and while he supported her she could stretch down and release the catch of the lower window. Within minutes his plan was safely accomplished. He then helped her through the larger window and within seconds we were safely inside.

The policeman did not linger. His dinner was more immediate in his mind. Thanking him, off he went and we soon followed, the house secured safely, and the dogs and ourselves together on the outside. Unfortunately, we did not return to that house again for, after so many months of being the only people interested in its purchase, someone else was now interested. Our own house had been on the market for a year with still no sign of a possible sale, so reluctantly I decided we would have to stay there until the demand for housing improved. Sadly, the opportunity for my mother and her sister to live with us never returned.

CHAPTER FIVE

Adapting to loss and fresh horizons

Apart from the dogs, we had a guinea pig called Joey in a long wooden cage in the back porch. We passed him frequently on the way into the garden and Willie had a special relationship with the small animal. She was just the right height to communicate in her own way and Joey's confined existence made him curious about any movement near his cage. He was old and when he eventually died the dogs missed him and Willie was very subdued as if she was grieving for the loss of the little creature. For the first time I realised that she was getting old, too, and when Heather finished school and went off to university Willie and Sebastian's companionship became even more precious.

The memories of that period are somewhat blurred as I was not finding my teaching job particularly rewarding. My views on the individuality of children with special needs differed so widely from that of my headmaster and one or two of the other staff that I relied not only on my dogs but other local organisations for enjoyment. My daughter and I had been members of the local Natural History Society since coming to the area but I now joined the Ramblers' Association and took a more active role in the local branch of the W.E.A. (Workers' Education Association). Now assistant to the secretary, the dogs and I regularly delivered notes to his home a good walking distance away. It made an enjoyable and regular walk for the three of us, but I knew that Willie was slowing down and there came a time when she preferred to be left at home.

I realised that I would soon have to adjust to being without Willie. Dogs leave a void which seems impossible at first to fill, and I have found that one frequently senses their presence for a considerable time after they have passed away. Perhaps it is just wishful thinking but like a person one has been very close to their spirit hangs around in a comforting sort of way until the need has faded.

The eventual sale of our house was quite an event. It sold within a week of the estate agent suggesting it might be the right time to put it back on the market, and my younger daughter who was on vacation at the time, with Sebastian for company, did most if not all of the search for a new home. I was only free in the evenings to view the places that she liked and thought I would appreciate, too. There was no chain of buyers and sellers that one experiences today, but property prices had just begun to increase. I was able to clear my mortgage and put a substantial down payment on the house I next chose. It was not occupied and I soon moved in. It was an attractive semi-detached with a safe fenced garden for Sebastian and drive in parking space for the car. There was an old shrub which had been trained up and over the front door and the beautiful passion flowers which appeared each year added to the charm of the mock Tudor frontage.

For some time prior to this move, Sebastian and I had made regular visits to a nursing home where I had a terminally ill friend. The staff allowed me to take the dog into his private room and on our way out I was asked to take him to visit some of the other residents. They loved putting a hand on his head, conveniently at the right height for bed bound patients, and I was told that his visits brought both joy and comfort. He was always quiet and I think he knew his presence was contributing to the wellbeing of those elderly men and women. After my friend passed away and my move to the new house, the visits ceased but Sebastian had revealed yet another aspect of his character.

I had for many years been a one parent family, the father of my two elder children who I loved dearly having left the country largely for political and cultural reasons. The marriage to the father of my youngest had not worked out, and I had always secretly hoped that one day my teenage love and I could be reunited. After years without contact, a long distance telephone friendship had been resumed, although our personal lives were unaffected.

In the middle of the very cold and snowy winter of 1978, I was enjoying the warmth of the downstairs room overlooking the garden and studying part of my geological collection when the telephone rang. It was an overseas call and my instinctive joy was abruptly shattered. The poor connection disclosed it was the brother of my dear friend phoning to tell me that he had died. Sebastian was always somewhere close and I do not know what I would have done without his large, solid and comforting presence beside me when I collapsed grief-stricken to the floor. I threw my arms around him and gave way to grief at this sudden unexpected end to many years of love and hope. Without my dog I would have been unable to continue with a life that had so often been a battle physically and mentally.

I struggled on to the end of the school year with a lot of compassion from my fellow teachers and including, surprisingly, the head teacher. He must have paved the way to the sabbatical year's leave I was offered, although I have no clear recollection of those months or my application and acceptance for an advanced course in special education at the University of Southampton.

At some stage, a young Canadian teacher briefly joined the school staff and she gave me the addresses of people to contact should I ever wish to teach in Canada. I had revisited British Columbia twice in recent years, staying with relatives and travelling on my own to learn more of the country of my birth, but I had given no serious thought to living there again. In my unsettled state of mind, I wrote to find out whether it was possible to obtain a teaching position but after a short correspondence there had been nothing constructive offered.

My year at university involved a daily train journey there and back, so I became accustomed to a very early start to each day, taking Sebastian out at 5.00 am for a good walk before often running to the railway station. They were pleasant walks when we seldom met another person, just the occasional cat on its way home from its nocturnal activities. It was becoming obvious that Sebastian was slowing down too. The vet said he was just getting old, and when he began preferring the garden to another long walk in the evening I had to accept that the years were passing and he had long outlived his old friend Zarka. His companionship became doubly important to me through this year of intensive study and research. He listened intently as so many dogs do when we had one-sided discussions on the events and problems of the day. Dogs cannot possibly understand what their owners are talking about so earnestly, but I am sure they derive a lot from the tone of voice and the variety of moods expressed whether happy, excited, thoughtful or sad, particularly when their lives have been so much a part of each other. When I finally had to say goodbye, I was prepared and resigned to once again losing a canine companion who had been both friend and support for so long.

CHAPTER SIX

Heading to Canada and very large paws

In September 1979, I returned to school full of new confidence and it was accepted that I was now looking for promotion and a new job. I had three very good interviews and had been short listed but each time a male applicant with lesser qualifications was selected. This experience was not new as I had a similar disappointment before entering the teaching profession. I had been short listed for the position of Assistant Editor to my Company's monthly gazette, decades earlier, and had been told that as I had a young family the nearest candidate, a man, would be more reliable!

For some time, I had realised that, in their own ways, all of my children were looking for overseas adventures and fresh opportunities. I began to give serious thought to perhaps finding myself alone with them all thousands of miles away. I applied for a teaching post in the West Indies but got no response, not surprisingly, as I had little knowledge beyond the English-speaking Caribbean and no knowledge of the language spoken on that particular island despite more than adequate qualifications for the job. I was still full of confidence, particularly due to my post-graduate study, but very lonely since losing Sebastian. Then out of the blue I heard from Canada, a large brown envelope containing an

Interim Teaching Certificate dropping through my letter box. It had taken so long to be issued that I had forgotten about it. Almost at the same time my old Morris Traveller 'died' and I found the expense of repair to a vehicle which was now regarded as a collectors' item well beyond my capacity. I now had to rely on colleagues for lifts to and from work, or use the very inadequate public transport. I was also rapidly approaching my fiftieth birthday.

Looking back through the eventful years that have passed since then I can only think that my subsequent actions were driven by hormonal change at a time when I was still suffering from a mixture of loss, disappointment, loneliness and hopeless dreams. During the spring of 1980, I put my house on the market, resigned from my teaching job, arranged for the possessions I wished to keep to be shipped to British Columbia, set my finances in order and booked a flight to Canada. I have been known for making rapid decisions throughout my life but this occurred in a little over three months. The house sold almost immediately. It was a charming little place where, in different circumstances, I could have lived happily for years. I made an enormous profit at the time as property values had risen in value in the few years I had lived there. I was therefore financially secure for the immediate future.

I was met in Vancouver by a much loved older brother. He and his wife offered me a home for as long as I wished, but I was determined to find a new teaching position wherever that might be. As soon as my goods arrived by sea I wished to be independent and to establish a new home of my own. Such wishes have consequences! I found work within weeks of my arrival, a remote teaching position on a First Nations

(Indian) Reserve. It was situated on an island off the British Columbian west coast many miles north of my brother's suburban home in Vancouver. He and his wife were both very supportive but concerned for my safety. They helped me to obtain the essentials I had been instructed to provide for life in an isolated community. We found my destination on a map and planned how I was to get there.

My new home by the sea

I had been given two options, a long sea journey by ferry which called at my destination once a week, or a flight by float plane. Given the short time before the start of the school term I opted for the latter and dropped my intention to await the arrival in Vancouver of my possessions from England. Instead, I found myself on the smallest plane I had ever imagined, with my two cases strapped to the seat beside me. There were three other passengers, two loggers returning to their forest camp somewhere up north who we dropped off halfway through our journey and a third quiet gentleman sitting virtually in the tail of the plane. I did not know he was there until we made our first flurried landing on a choppy sea and we were told to get out on a pontoon to stretch our legs while the pilot took on fuel. My fascination in the pilot's tasks had helped dispel my initial fear of the flight as the cockpit was open and just in front of me. He had a map of the area to which he frequently referred before he found the forestry camp, and occasionally turned to share a joke with the men.

When we touched down at our final destination the sea was very restless and the little plane rose and fell as the pilot secured it to a heaving pontoon and helped me out, depositing my cases on a surface wet with spray. I think they would have slid into the sea if the other passenger had not come forward to help. Without his assistance I could not have bridged the gap between what turned out to be two pontoons that opened and closed ominously in the turbulent water. Only then could we reach the safety of a small open boat with an outboard engine apparently awaiting our arrival. Twenty minutes later I had reached the place I was to regard as home for the next three years.

It was an equally eventful landing but on a more stable pontoon with the wharf high above as it was apparently low tide. I was met by the smiling Chief of the community who, having asked me if I could climb the almost perpendicular ladder unaided, seized both my heavy cases and ran up the steps. I followed more slowly, wondering for the hundredth time why I had embarked on such an adventure.

Minutes later I was sitting in the cab of possibly the only truck on the island bouncing up a dirt track where rocks stuck out of the steep hill and pot holes were as much part of the surface as the piles of loose pebbles. We were also surrounded by numerous large dogs, barking, snarling and jumping at the wheels and sides of the truck. The driver ignored them completely and why none ended under the wheels I do not know. At last I reached my temporary accommodation, three enormous basement rooms under a 'teacherage' which was home to another couple. The wife brought me a mug of tea and left me to unpack. I think I just unrolled the sleeping bag I had been instructed to bring and laid it on the wooden bed frame, and sat down and felt completely lonely and lost. I need not have worried.

Isolated communities welcome any newcomer even if they reject the very same person at a later date, and before I had time to really feel sorry for myself, another teacher appeared, inviting me to an evening meal. She lived just down the hill and would become a great friend, the nearest to my age among the other staff who were on average ten to twenty years younger. After the meal during which I learnt a lot about the school, staff and the Reserve, I was collected by two other teachers who took me on a tour of the community village and showed me the Band Store where the necessities of life were purchased, mainly food, but essentials such as light bulbs and toiletries. Such things I was told were brought in from Vancouver by barge, so depended completely on good weather.

That introductory walk was relatively short as there were only two dirt roads, one close to the sea and the other further inland, connected by shorter tracks every so often. The houses were built on piles. This was rain forest country, and I soon learnt that the largely boarded up spaces underneath each house were mainly used as dens by feral dogs. I had never heard of a feral dog before, but there was much I did not understand as my companions pointed out one feature after another as we walked. Then we were suddenly confronted by a lady with an armful of puppies. She said their mother had disappeared and the first she knew about them was when they found their way out from under her house. She did not want them so they would likely starve. They all looked pretty fat to me although I would soon find out that they were all infested with worms! Most feral dogs lived and died in the same condition.

What did interest me was that she was so keen for us to take them. I asked my companions what was the school position regarding pets and they both assured me that there were no restrictions on keeping pets, although they seemed surprised and a bit doubtful when I chose one of the adorable fluffy creatures and said I would like to have it. The older of my companions said it had enormous paws which indicated it would grow into a very big dog, but having been accustomed to my dear old Great Dane I ignored the comment and so we returned to my new accommodation with the puppy. I decided to call him Sam.

It was late summer, 1980. I was about to start on yet another challenging period of my life. The puppy was only one small part of that challenge, but without his companionship I am not sure how or if I could have survived the following years.

CHAPTER SEVEN

Rainforest country

I found I had a puppy who had no idea of feeding himself. Because he would readily suck milk from my fingers I realised he would have to be hand fed for some time. Warm bread and milk proved adequate. What did surprise me although I did not question it at the time, was that within a matter of days colleagues provided me with a shallow feeding bowl, a little red collar, a lead, worming tablets, and even a length of cord so that when Sam became more steady on his wobbly feet he could venture further from my side to explore the unknown world outside our basement dwelling. Once the worm problem was solved and he learnt to eat on his own he flourished and we began to establish the bond that would last for the remainder of his life.

I soon learnt why Sam's immediate needs had been provided so promptly. Among the advice given from all and sundry on my own safe survival in my new island home, was the strict instruction to keep away from the rain forest. It surrounded us on every side and reached almost to the water's edge along the coast, and although it was dense and dark, it looked very inviting to me. I have always loved trees and the landscape I had seen from the air seemed very attractive. Living here meant that I would need to speedily acquire items that each had to be shipped in by barge. I heard numerous sad accounts of teachers who had lost pets in the past. Some had arrived with their own cats or dogs, but many had been given puppies as I had been. All seemed to have died, disappeared or been killed by feral dogs or wolves. I would soon realise too, that it was only the strongest or most ferocious feral dogs who were likely to survive in what was a very dangerous environment. Others were just lucky or more intelligent and managed to outlive the majority.

The more I heard the more determined I became that I would keep my little dog safe. Sam was never allowed outside unless I was there and he had to remain on his lead. I checked the immediate vicinity for signs of other dogs and was constantly alert when outside, but the dogs roamed in packs and during daylight hours they normally kept their distance from human presence. They had good reason to be wary as I gradually found out.

Meanwhile, I had plenty to occupy my time and thoughts: a new job, a fascinating culture, a delightful group of children to teach and new friends. I also had to establish my place in an extraordinary hierarchy that had developed among a group of teachers and other professionals who had chosen to temporarily isolate themselves often far from home and from situations that they had found untenable. Collectively, and including a small contingent of the RCMP (the Royal Canadian Mounted Police) although ours had no horses or cars, and also a handful of church and hospital staff, we incomers were a very small minority within a much larger First Nations' island community. I found the latter both welcoming and friendly but the complex interactions within the structure of the school were hard for me to understand.

Despite being Canadian by birth, I had almost no experience or understanding of Canadian society, so the frictions among my new professional colleagues were not straightforward to understand. Fortunately I found great satisfaction within the confines of my classroom and largely managed to keep apart from the tensions that affected the lives and leisure times of many of my colleagues.

In my new island home, I was able to walk home for lunch and to see Sam, and to take him outside for a short walk morning and evening. As a result, as the weeks went by, I began to recognise and be recognised by many members of the Indigenous community. After all, I was the new teacher from England who had come over 4,500 miles to work in their school! The Elders were often standing in their doorways and would call out greetings in English to which I would gladly respond. Many of the men I met were curious about my arrival on the island and even more interested in my dog.

When Sam was little he had very clear lines of dark hair on his face and legs which contrasted sharply with his otherwise creamy colouring. I looked in vain among the feral dogs for one that might be genetically linked to him. They represented a surprising variety. Some still carried their previous winter's coat in dirty matted chunks clinging to their sides until they managed to shed the irritating burden. Sam had two distinct coats, a soft white wool close to his skin which I combed out in huge quantities each year and a protective coarser longer hair of a totally different texture and colour on top. My First Nation friends said he was a husky/wolf and I accepted this.

Sam grew rapidly, turning from a cuddly puppy to a lean muscular and very active animal in a very short space of time.

When I first left the Reserve for urgent dental treatment off-island, I had to entrust him to the care of other teachers who were part of the small group who shared a similar outlook on life to my own. Sam managed to destroy their protective inner door which acted as a screen from the black flies that plagued the village each summer. They blamed themselves for thinking that he was still too small to try to escape outside when they were not in the house. The damage was most unfortunate but also repairable as was our friendship. However, Sam was already showing that he was growing into a powerful dog.

Sam and I did not stay in our basement apartment for long. The school administration knew that I had shipped some of my possessions from England but I still had no idea when they would arrive in Vancouver. My brother offered to see them through Customs and then arrange for their onward transport by barge to the island. So I was allocated a duplex in the centre of the village. I had never heard of a duplex but It turned out to be one half of a large wooden bungalow. A remarkably thin partition wall separated Sam and myself from the First Nations' family living next door. After my basement rooms at the top of Teacher Hill it was wonderfully spacious, and I looked forward to the arrival of my possessions.

It was quite an event when I was informed that the goods had been off loaded on the wharf as I was the first teacher to arrive in the community with so many worldly goods. These were delivered on the truck by the father of one of the children in my class and he and his companion were both astonished and curious at the many crates and boxes, and their contents and weight. There was a great deal of friendly banter as they hauled in boxes of books and my metal cabinets of geological specimens, cases and trunk. Over a pot of tea and homemade cookies I promised to later show them the contents, further strengthening the friendships Sam and I had made already within the community. I had never tried to make cookies before but now I found I needed to have a continuous supply. As soon as I started cooking, the tops of little heads with eager eyes were peeping through my window, knowing that they would be given some. The children loved Sam but I resisted their pleas to let him out to play with them.

It was shortly after I had distributed my possessions around the main room that Sam committed the only real crime of his life. Along with minimal but adequate furniture and the largest noisiest oil furnace I have ever seen the main room had an inexpensive carpet square. One day while I was at school Sam had found some interesting smell at the edge of the carpet and had begun to chew. I had anticipated a puppy's teething needs and provided him with an old shoe and other bits I had found washed up on the shore, but whatever was on the edge of that carpet proved irresistible. I came home to find that he had chewed away not one but several chunks down one side. I was so shocked that it is the only time he provoked me to anger, wondering how on earth I would explain away the damage and whether I would have to pay for a replacement. That evening after much thought I got out my metre rule, a piece of chalk and some carpet shears, fortunately all part of the things I had thought I might need when packing up in England, and carefully measured a six inch strip (15 cms) down the damaged side. Then somewhat laboriously I cut it off, trimmed away any shaggy threads, and hid it away in my trunk. I moved the furniture around so that all the carpet edges would be protected from further puppy predation. It worked and there were too many events occurring all around me to give it further thought. When I moved again some months later and the inventory was checked no one noticed that the carpet square had turned into a carpet rectangle, and indeed the latter shape suited the room much better!

Meanwhile my walks with Sam were becoming more adventurous. At the weekends when I had plenty of time I began to explore further afield as by now I was familiar with the whole village and many of the residents. There was an old logging road at the far end of the settlement winding steeply up the rocky hillside and where the few houses ended I found I had a new world to explore. The sea, with a glorious view of other islands and the mountains on the British Columbian mainland in the distance, lay far below me on one side with rocks, shrub and forest rising from the edge of the track

Bringing in logs for my burner, c.1981

on the other. I seldom met anyone and I soon realised that Sam could run free away from the village, which was good for us both. I could enjoy the many new plants, mosses and lichens everywhere, the birds and their unfamiliar calls, and the sight of distant boats for ours was a fishing community. When I eventually got the courage to walk literally to the end of the road I found myself in a different world.

Sam on the shore

At some time in the past, a reservoir had been created where a stream cascaded down into the sea. The low wall built at one end was the only apparent link to the logged mountain on the far side and it took a brave heart and good balance to walk across between a swampy area amidst forest and the flooded valley beyond. Cedar trees had been left standing so that the water was dark stained and forbidding and here and there the ancient trunks of once majestic trees were still visible. It was an eerie place but to me quite magical, so quiet and so far removed from life's many problems. Sam was a little uncertain of these new surroundings and stayed close to me. Perhaps he felt as I did that we were not alone, that there were eyes watching from the dense undergrowth on every side but I did not feel threatened then or at any time when we went there on future walks.

Sam was growing fast. He was no longer round and cuddly but long legged, thin and muscular, and very active when off his lead. Everyone said he was going to be very big but I had no idea of his potential strength until one day I tethered him to the ferry's metal steps. These were wheeled into place at high tide so that passengers could disembark or reach the deck on the outgoing journey. It was always a busy scene of comings and goings and a weekly event for many people. On this occasion I was also there to bid a friend goodbye. Many teachers could not cope with the isolation or left suddenly for health or other reasons.

I had moved only a short distance away from Sam when I was called back by excited voices. Sam, not used to being tied, had apparently tried to follow me, and had already moved the huge wheeled structure from its position by the ferry. Fortunately it was not being used at that time. From then on Sam became very well known to some of the crew, and as we would both use the ferry many times in the future it served me well. I had been very embarrassed at the incident but after the initial consternation there was nothing but admiration for the powerful strength of my island dog.

Unfortunately there were others who took note of his future potential. One Sunday morning, very early when the village was quiet, Sam and I were taking our carefree morning walk when, out of nowhere, a pack of dogs launched an attack. It happened so suddenly I did not have time to think or even feel fear. Clinging to Sam's lead I was immediately knocked off my feet and all I could later recall was the snarling mob above me, seemingly fighting each other as they tried to get at Sam. Fortunately at the time of the attack, two men possibly returning from a fishing trip, came around the corner to my aid and, within seconds, a couple of the teaching staff also joined the fray. The feral dogs, vicious among themselves are very wary of humans, and a few savage kicks and blows drove them off and we were rescued. Without the intervention I might not have survived.

I was informed within hours that it was essential that Sam should be neutered as otherwise we would now be in constant danger. The feral dogs had sensed a potential rival in their midst and, in a world of survival of the strongest and the fittest, my Sam had no safe place. I was given time off to take the southbound ferry to the nearest kennels at the northern end of Vancouver island and a vet where the procedure could be performed. Sam stayed at the kennels and I put up at the only hotel, places which would become very familiar to us both in the future as I could leave him safely at the kennels while I visited family overseas during school holidays. After a few days I was able to collect a rather subdued dog and board the northbound ferry once again for the place I now considered home. Sam had to travel on the car deck several steep gangways below but there was always a willing member of the crew to help me navigate the steps and then secure him to the longer chain I had obtained to give him more freedom of movement. I could visit him from time to time on the voyage north to reassure him but after that first double journey he just took every new experience in his stride.

Sam's stitches were removed by our resident doctor in the basement of the little hospital overlooking the sea and his recovery was uneventful. I still walked him on his lead through the village but he began to have more freedom on the shore and from then on he was ignored by the feral dogs we met, even enjoying short friendships with younger animals although they never survived for long. I was gradually becoming aware that dogs had little value here, as in many societies, and that to regard them as members of the family as I had always done was unusual. The fact that most dogs had no owner, died of starvation, were shot, or regularly rounded up for culling was just a way of life in this remote community, but was very hard for me to adjust to. Children who had cherished a puppy and played with it for a few months were temporarily upset but they soon forgot. Sam was the exception. I think he was admired by many and accepted by all.

CHAPTER EIGHT

Cabin by the ocean

After some months living in the heart of the village I learnt from two of my colleagues that they were planning to leave and they thought I might be interested in their accommodation. I immediately applied for the tenancy when it became available. I believe I had no competition as the other teaching staff enjoyed socialising with neighbours and the convenience of homes close to school. They all thought the site was too isolated for safety and possibly knew of its dilapidation. Possibly they could foresee some of the problems I might face. However, sometimes ignorance can be an asset.

Sam and I moved in to what I believe had once been a floating home or float house. Now it was beached just above high tide level and supported on wooden piles dug into the coarse sand and gravel of the last walkable section of shore before the edge of the rain forest met the rocky coast and sea. It was approached by a long wooden causeway as at high tide the ground became saturated and the cabin would have been inaccessible. A cable for electricity and a water pipe linked the float house to village amenities, but drainage was piped directly to the sea. I would soon discover the inefficiencies of the latter as Pacific storms could roll extremely heavy items over such pipes which, when broken, immediately became blocked with gravel. The location and views seemed ideal as I could gaze out over other tree-clad islands that flanked this section of British Columbia's famed Inner Passage. Bald headed eagles would sit on the rocks and driftwood in front of my kitchen window, ravens strutted on the wooden shingles of my float-house roof and out to sea I would glimpse the flash of a leaping fish or the occasional distant spout of a whale.

Sam could at last run free without the restraint of a rope attached to his collar, leaping from the walkway just outside our only door and racing off to explore the delights of the shore while I followed at a more leisurely pace. I never allowed him to be out there alone. The feral dogs kept closer to the village, possibly for safety although as, from time to time when they were rounded up and shot, it proved anything but safe, but I was relieved to meet them far less often now when out with Sam.

The island shore was an endless source of delight to us both. Every receding tide left a new assortment of flotsam and jetsam, and I soon found that I could salvage many useful household items if I was patient enough to wait, including a broom, a bucket and a doormat. Looking back, I marvel at the items lost overboard and deposited on distant shores still in relatively good condition. If Sam had been the sort of animal who loved balls I would have gained a regular supply from those spotted during our daily shore excursions. In fact, he preferred the long slimy strands of kelp which were abundant, a half buried ragged jacket or old boot that he could excavate or tug free. There were other far from savoury items which he would discover as the months passed by.

My other joy and a constant source of pleasure for Sam when I had the time to go so far was the rain forest. It began where the track to the village ended, wrapping itself around the remains of the shore before rocky outcrops prevented human passage except by swimming or boat. We had to walk to the end of the shore before clambering up a slope of compacted rocks and earth to reach what was generally known as the old Indian trail. I would later learn that it had connected the original site of the village to its present location. Early European settlers had brought virulent contagious diseases to the former village. Smallpox had decimated the population during the 1860s and a new site for the survivors had been established.

At the time I was still unaware of that tragic episode from the not too distant past, and the long shadow of colonial history still affecting people's lives and opportunities today. Instead, I felt I was entering a world of enchantment. The narrow trail led into a dimly lit place of forest giants, cedars, hemlock and others I could not then recognise, their lower branches draped with curtains of moss reaching down to water saturated hollows between the rotten remnants of tree stumps, vegetation and bush. It was impossible to proceed very far before meeting the massive moss covered remains of fallen trees sometimes on the forest floor but sometimes waist high as they lay snagged and suspended by nearby trees. When I first ventured into the forest, Sam was still a puppy and I had to lift him onto the top of one such fallen forest giant, scramble up beside him and then lift him down again. He was too inquisitive to wait on that first adventuresome trip and was frightened when he rolled down the far side but as he grew, he could reach the top on his own and easily leap down while I cautiously followed.

Sam never left the trail even when the vegetation became temporarily less dense. The forest was a mysterious silent place, the only sounds an occasional plop of water or the cracking sound of some unseen animal moving past but I never felt threatened in any way with Sam beside me. Whatever larger wildlife there was kept quietly hidden. Only the giant banana slug ventured to cross our path, usually where there were boggy hollows that seasonally supported the skunk cabbage plant. Its early shoots made their vivid and startling appearance and seemed to light up the gloom of the forest floor before their penetrating odour warned of their presence. It was a strangely beautiful plant, one of many magical things we would encounter on our walks.

Sam was fascinated by the sea but the first indication I had that he could swim was a day when a cruiseship, with its rails lined with passengers hoping to get a view of the village and the residents, coincided with our own walk down on the shore. The boat was too far out to see clearly, particular with my eyesight, but voices carry and, much to my consternation Sam, decided it was something worth swimming out to investigate. Ignoring my calls he dashed into the sea and began to swim, the first time I had seen him do more than get his feet wet. He swam on and on until I could barely see his head above the water and I thought I had finally lost him. Somehow, he must have sensed it was a fruitless journey and finally turned back and headed for the shore. I wonder if he became a detail in the holiday memories of those passengers curious about life on these remote shores?

Sam frightened me on one other similar occasion shortly afterwards and then found other more interesting things to do. I was offered and bought a clinker built wooden rowing boat that opened fresh possibilities of exploring the immediate coast line. Thinking that Sam would react as most dogs do and settle down in the stern as I sculled my way past previously hidden islets and coves, I was disappointed. He preferred the water to the boat, and although he followed me swimming sturdily I was too concerned for his whereabouts and safety to fully enjoy such adventures.

I should not have worried as I later learnt that this part of British Columbia is known for its distinctive sea or coastal wolves that are a subspecies of the grey wolf. Sam was probably descended from these island wolves who are great swimmers, covering long distances as the packs move from island to island. One clear moonlight night as I looked out from my window, I saw such a pack following the edge of the sea in front of my cabin. I was told that they were probably on their way to the village dump at the opposite end of the settlement. It was a thrilling sight but tinged with the knowledge that, if they met the feral village dogs, only the strongest adults of these fascinating and still misunderstood animals would survive the night.

Sam had made a number of friends within the community, particularly among people we saw frequently. These included my immediate neighbours who supported themselves and made a living from the sea. During the salmon season I became accustomed to seeing families cooking around fires on the shore where they would gut the fish and fix them to wooden frames to sizzle in the heat. During food preparation discarded bits of salmon were draped over a line nearby and I enjoyed watching from my windows as the bald headed eagles swooped down to retrieve this largesse.

My cabin on the shore in the winter months

Sam and I benefitted, too. One morning we were presented with a newly caught salmon. It was offered to Sam and clutching it in the middle with his teeth he carried it back into the cabin. I could see a tasty opportunity too. Fortunately, by now Sam had learnt to surrender many unsuitable things he found, so he let me remove his prize which I washed, cut into chunks and put into my freezer. Thanking the fisherman later for this gift assured a ready supply of salmon from then on, a rich source of protein for Sam and myself. Many types of sea food had great cultural and nutritional value and were still abundant within the community in the early 1980s, but salmon was always my favourite. During my island years, I am sure salmon contributed both to my health and Sam's fitness and growing maturity.

CHAPTER NINE

Pacific storm

Our closeness to the sea was an ever present reality, and indeed a potential threat although it was many months before I gave it much thought. High tides and storms could transform the aspect of our shoreline overnight. On one occasion we found an enormous tree stump with its roots still attached embedded in the gravel half way between the cabin and the forest. It reared above us, draped with bits of fishing net, rope and seaweed, and looked as if it had been there for years. It remained a landmark for many months, a natural art form that I sketched, photographed and explored for it snagged and later discarded many strange objects brought in by high tides. It was also a wonderful lookout for perching solitary birds and a source of daily exploration for a curious dog passing by. If it had crashed into my float house, what a different story this might have been! Fortunately, that alarming thought never occurred to me until after it had departed on its next maritime voyage as it had arrived, during one night, unobserved.

An extremely low tide was a much rarer occurrence, at least in my experience. One weekend morning when Sam and I had time for more leisurely walks than on school days I found the sea level had dropped many feet (and metres!)

Tree roots washed by winter storms, c.1982

– something I had never previously observed. A completely alien normally submerged marine world was exposed as we now stood on the edge of a cliff, rocks sloping down to a new level of sand and gravel. Sam ran excitedly to and fro until he found a gap in the rocks where the ground formed a less precipitous slope. Without hesitation he bounded down to explore and, feeling that where he went I could safely follow, I soon found myself in a very strange environment. It seemed cold and utterly remote, with jagged rocks thrusting up through a much sandier floor than up at normal shore level. It was as if I had reached the ocean floor on foot!

There were piles of orange brown sea stars, better known as starfish, clustered around the base of the rocks in such abundance that I could have filled numerous buckets with ease, but I was stopped in my tracks by the most enormous purple sea star I have ever seen. It lay there, a glistening fleshy creature about seventy centimetres across like something out of science fiction. Fortunately it was motionless for I might have reacted unwisely had it moved. Sam decided at that moment to return to his more familiar surroundings and without hesitation and feeling completely unnerved I followed. There had been other unusual creatures down there which normally I would have found fascinating but fear and the safety I found in Sam's presence made for a hurried departure from this rarely exposed intertidal zone. It was an experience I remember with awe and almost disbelief but it was never repeated.

Sam's greatest find, but certainly not mine, was a wolf skin. Its origin was a mystery as the local First Nations honour the animal alongside the raven, killer whale (orca), bear and others in their rich belief system. For many people, the wolf represents loyalty and has the courage and strength of the hunter. Sam's find had lost its dignity. He dragged the skin home for almost a mile. It had not been cleaned or prepared in any way and had possibly been in the sea for some time. It was revolting but Sam loved it. I tried to dispose of it several times but on each occasion he discovered it afresh until one stormy night when the waves were perilously close to the cabin's walkway. It was a relief when I realised it had finally been carried out to sea once more, a more fitting place for the region's mysterious sea wolves.

It was not unusual for me to go out of the cabin after dark with Sam. Normally, he came back within minutes and I enjoyed the creaks and sounds of our surroundings as I waited for his return. One night after an unusually high tide I slipped on the wet wood, hitting my head and losing consciousness. The next thing I remember was Sam looming over me and licking my face. Still semi-conscious I found his collar, pulled myself up into a sitting position and somehow with his help managed to crawl the few metres back to the door. I do not recall anything further until the following morning when I found myself on the floor beside him as I tried to remember what had happened. It was the only night my float house door remained unlocked. Usually a heavy bolt and a padlock and chain, together with Sam's presence, made me feel utterly secure.

Waves outside my window

The episode left me with a horrendous black eye which went through numerous colour changes before it disappeared. The bruising attracted both concern and later considerable merriment from community members who knew me, and also from teaching colleagues I met, until I had been checked as able to teach by our resident doctor. Fortunately I was none the worse for my adventure but it gave me a lasting wariness of wooden walkways and an even deeper affection for my dog. Without Sam's attempts at reviving me and his assistance in my regaining the shelter of our home anything might have happened. In this isolated lifestyle I had opted for, far away from family who I knew had their own concerns about my well-being, I had become hugely reliant upon my massive wolf-like companion.

Living so close, indeed, almost on the sea left me with many incredible memories. I had always loved the sea and had a deep respect for her many moods – tranquil, playful, boisterous or destructive. The remains of trees and driftwood piled below my kitchen window had gradually accumulated and would brush against the cabin at high tide but never caused me much concern. They seemed more of a protective layer than a danger particularly when high tides caused waves to slap across the kitchen window. The ever changing shoreline, sounds and scents were unforgettable, but one experience was also very frightening and made me aware that my rented cabin home that I had grown to love was not the idyllic place I imagined.

One night a Pacific storm brought waves and huge pieces of drift wood not only perilously close to the cabin but right up to my walls and windows. I was too afraid to go to bed and sat in the kitchen with Sam. Perhaps we both sensed that this time, things were different. The cabin shuddered with the impact of the huge waves and water began to trickle through the delapidated kitchen wall. There were also signs of leakage through the floor although it was being absorbed by the heavy matting on which Sam usually slept. I wondered what would happen if that wall were breached. My walkway was already under water and impassable and the ferocious wind, in any case, would have made escape impossible through the one outside door.

My mind worked nonstop, one hand on Sam, strengthened by his reassuring presence, planning through that terrifying night, waiting for the worst and determined to survive. I viewed the kitchen table, and its sturdy wooden structure as a potential raft. Sam was such a strong swimmer. I decided to tether him with a long rope to one of its solid legs and looped another rope along the edge to hold on to myself if the cabin collapsed and we were swept out to sea. There was just a chance we could save ourselves. It was hour after hour of fear. Fortunately the cabin wall and floor, damaged and leaking, survived the night. So did we.

Next morning the shore told a different story. Half way to the forest at the end of the cove an entire house had been washed up by the waves. The walls had folded inwards on the wooden platform that had once held floor and deck, and the roof still rested in its entirety on the broken remains. The metal stovepipe with its cone shaped cap, so like that of my cabin, still protruded crookedly from the wooden shakes (roof tiles), and I could only marvel at the twin light fitting on the gable end miraculously still in place, the bulbs unbroken.

I was able to examine the washed up house in detail as it blocked our daily walks along the shore, and it was only when Sam found a safe way of crossing the tilted roof and I carefully followed that our longer walks could be resumed. I learnt in due course that the building had been carried by the strong currents across the inlet from another island, some miles away. Fortunately, the owners were safe. Eventually those sad remains were burnt one day while I was at school, but I realised how easily such a tragedy could have involved myself and Sam.

By now I had been teaching on the island for almost three years. I had seen many changes of staff and other personnel, and said goodbye to the majority of the friends I had made during that time. The school's administrator had already left with his family and had offered me another teaching position in a less isolated place, but the decision to move was finally made following advice from one of my own family. When Claudia Ruth came to visit with her two young children her advice was that if I did not leave soon I would be there for ever – 'bushed' being the appropriate term! Having so enjoyed watching my grandson playing with the rowing boat and exploring on the beach, I had mixed feelings about the thought of leaving. It was also true that I was beginning to accept the many traumas that occurred around me as readily as I enjoyed the many happy occasions within community life, and had no real desire to move on.

The new proposed teaching position certainly had much to offer. I would be near old friends and within driving distance of a niece and family and their small town, St Albert, in Alberta. I was assured that the area in which I would be living would be suitable for Sam, and so the decision to move was made. Whether it was a wise one, looking back over many years, I still do not know.

Dorothy and Sebastian, Dorset – c.1975

Sam at three and a half months by my door – 1980

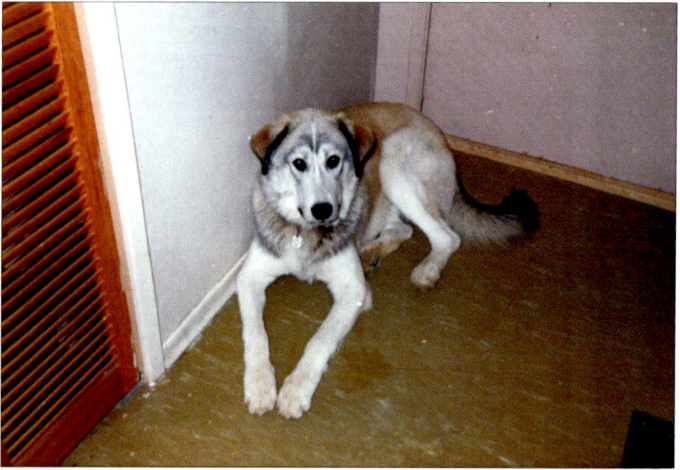

Sam showing his wolf markings

Sam with one of his toys from the sea – c.1981

Dorothy and Sam – mid 1980s

Sam and Gypsybella, Alberta, Canada – mid 1980s

Claudia Ruth and Sam, Alberta – mid 1980s

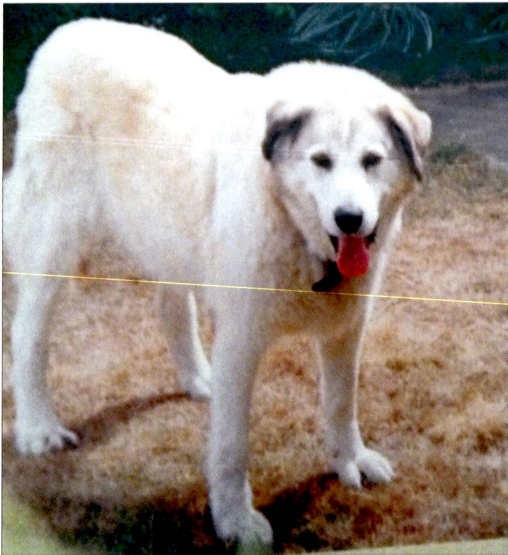

Sam in his summer coat, Duncan – early 1990s

Aburisa, Duncan, Vancouver Island, Canada – 1998

Bramble in the garden, West Yorkshire – c.2006

Leo and his friend Tiny, Yorkshire – 2018

Leo, West Yorkshire, 2018

CHAPTER TEN

Alberta and the need for a cat

At the end of the school year in the summer of 1983, I arranged for my possessions to be shipped once more by barge to Vancouver. A few days later Sam and I said goodbye to our seashore home and made the by now familiar six hour ferry journey to the northern tip of Vancouver Island. A friend, Wendy, who had already left some months previously arranged to meet the ferry with a hired van, a U-haul. The three of us then travelled down island, took another ferry across to Vancouver on the mainland and went to the warehouse where the barge had off-loaded my goods. These had increased considerably in quantity during my island years and trunks now filled the floor space of the van causing us concern for Sam's comfort while travelling. We need not have worried. Ever adaptable, he leapt onto the trunks and settled down, apparently content to see the road ahead over our heads.

It was a long drive, through the Rockies, leaving behind British Columbia, the province of my birth, and then travelling across the adjoining province of Alberta. The first time we made a convenience stop for Sam we were both very concerned about letting him roam free at such a high altitude, where the scenery was exquisitely beautiful, and the air so pure it took my breath away. I felt that our apparently empty surroundings might tempt him to go off exploring after being confined for hours in such a cramped space. As we stayed by the van he soon realised that no walk was involved and came back at speed, sprang up onto what must have been a very uncomfortable place to lie, and we continued on our way.

Eventually we drew up at a travel lodge where we booked in for the night. Much to my consternation the man at reception told us curtly we could not take such a large dog to our room but as I began to argue a warning kick from Wendy told me to leave the arrangements to her. I realised why soon after we gained access to our room. She had quickly assessed the layout of the building when we took Sam back to the van and went to collect him almost immediately, returning by the back entrance she had noted. We feared that he would start one of his prolonged and penetrating wolf howls if left alone too long. However, he settled down in a corner while we made a hot drink, ate a snack and retired to our beds exhausted. I was amazed at Wendy's resilience in driving the U-haul such long distances with relatively short breaks for food and rest, but my time in Canada had already made me realise that a number of my colleagues had acquired an utterly different set of life skills to my own. Many I would myself experience and adopt in the ensuing years, but at that time I had much to learn.

We left at early light, hoping that Sam had not left hair on the poor quality floor covering where he had slept. Usually I groomed him frequently, especially during the warmer months as his undercoat of cream coloured wool shed everywhere and often included the longer darker coarse hairs of his outer coat. Since leaving our island home there had been no time for such brushing and combing activities which I had found essential and which he enjoyed. Arriving at our destination in St. Albert, Alberta, where my niece gave us the key to a house she had found and rented on my behalf, we unloaded my things with the help of my nephew in law. Wendy was anxious to start her homeward journey, to return the U-haul on time and go home to her husband, so after some refreshments and a short rest, I sadly watched her depart. Sam and I were left to settle in together.

I recall little of that first night apart from waking suddenly to a thundering noise that shook the house and nearly frightened me out of my wits. It turned out next day that the house and yard – I already thought of it as a promising space for a garden – was right beside a railway line. Such rail tracks became a prominent feature for Sam and myself during the next six years as, paradoxically, it was the safest place for Sam to have his daily exercise. Most of the small prairie towns in Alberta grew up around the junction of a north/south and east/west line largely used by freight trains. These could have two engines and pull as many as an hundred waggons. They carried bells or whistles which were sounded at roughly mile intervals when approaching a small settlement where a track crossed the line. The trains travelled slowly so crossing the lines required being very patient and prepared for a long wait. However, trains were infrequent and could be heard many miles away. Their sound carried on the rails long before being able to detect the bell or whistle.

When my father first came to Canada, in the early 1900s, he had been a member of a railroad construction gang and he had worked his way up to the position of surveyor with the

Canadian National Railways. That personal link was always present in my mind while Sam bounded ahead, investigating the embankment on either side of the track. The scenery and wildlife varied through each year and while Sam enjoyed the freedom I treasured the solitude. We never met another walker and on the odd occasions our walk coincided with the passing of a train I revelled in the cheery calls from the cab and even occasionally a cheeky little blast from the whistle.

After some months I was able to buy my own property in the small town of Morinville, appropriately placed for my new school that was situated about twelve miles away across the prairie. As most of the teachers lived in the same area a mini bus took those who could not drive there each morning. The return was not easy as we had to wait until the last teacher was free to leave so the working days became rather stretched. But life was generally not as good as I had expected. We teachers were not made welcome locally due to historic antipathies between the settlement and their Plains Cree neighbours. Some of the latter also resented that they had to employ us to teach in their school: they were still reliant on non-Indigenous teachers while community members gained their own professional qualifications, now that responsibility for education had been handed from the government to Indigenous communities. Meanwhile the senior school managers seemed determined to get value for money from their brought in teachers. Gone were the days of being welcomed into private homes on the Reserve as I had become accustomed out on the west coast. Unfortunately, the distrust shown to us was also visible in relationships within their own community. As these memories focus on my years with dogs, I will not say much about my new teaching situation except to say that, as in most situations, there were positive and also difficult aspects, some of which I never fully understood and others I only came to understand in the ensuing years.

As part of the teaching and mentoring programme, we each had a classroom assistant and my first one was a lovely lady of my own age. Her husband worked on a trap line, securing both food and pelts as a living. When I first organised my classroom she carefully fastened various cultural objects to the classroom entrance which she explained would ward off evil and keep us safe. These traditional artefacts included a long-stemmed pipe, a bunch of sweet grass and eagle feathers. I did not understand their significance at the time but I felt she only had my well-being in mind. We became great friends within the confines of the classroom. As always, I found the children delightful despite the problems which sadly some of them would always have.

Away from school the teachers, many with their own families, shared interests that invariably included cats, for where there are grain silos on the Canadian prairies there are also abundant mice. We formed our own little community, something I would find extremely comforting in the difficult years that lay ahead for us all. Soon after arrival, I had to arrange a visit to a vet so that Sam could have the legally required injections and while there the subject of cats arose.

My first rented home in Alberta was infested by mice and I found mouse traps everywhere, something I found most distasteful having kept mice as a child and later I had them as classroom pets, alongside rabbits, hamsters and budgerigars. My new house had no little furry visitors but I had been assured they would move in when cold weather arrived. Very aware of the environment Sam and I had left behind and that he could be genetically prone to regard cats as potential food, the vet put my mind at rest. Sam had a gentle temperament, was happy and well fed, and the vet thought that the half grown cat he had in mind, to deal with the mouse problem, would not only be a companion but could take care of itself. He was correct in his assumptions.

When I first introduced the tabby to Sam he was sleeping happily on the kitchen floor. Raising his head with interest as I opened the hamper, I was horrified when she launched herself at him spitting with anger, probably because she had been cooped up too long. He had never seen a cat and she went straight for his nose, giving him a nasty scratch. He just got up and shook himself, towering over her surprised at this creature that I had brought home. After such an unpromising start, she probably slunk off to explore the new house but they would become lifetime friends. This companionship became very important due to the unusual elements of my new teaching post.

There seemed to be several conflicting factions on the Reserve that affected decision making and general peace of mind. Somewhere an idea arose that, by requiring us all to attend regular retreats away from school and home, the experience would have a healing effect within the community. With hindsight, the brutal legacies of colonial treatment had such traumatic effects upon successive generations that forms of cultural healing were needed to allow for practical, material and spiritual recovery to take place. But for most of the teachers who, myself included, entered Indigenous education in the 1980s, with little to no historical knowledge of what European settlement had meant for Canada's earlier inhabitants, the compulsory attendance at retreats was just another demand upon our time, energy and commitment. We were not always willing learners.

Often with little warning, teachers and classroom assistants would be obliged to travel by coach or air hundreds or even thousands of miles to some destination to take part in communal gatherings. This was very disruptive to teachers' lives, having to leave husbands, wives, children or, in my case pets, at short notice for very long weekends away. I was fortunate as the teenage daughter of a colleague who lived nearby volunteered to look after Sam and the cat I had named Gypsybella. Other colleagues faced practical problems that were harder to resolve.

The retreats sometimes involved attending sessions that seemed unrelated to either teaching or the Reserve's beliefs and cultural practices. However, they did allow time for some very interesting and enjoyable experiences for a few of us, particularly as these trips introduced me to new places both in Canada and down in the United States, and also the fascinating cultural diversity of Indigenous groups that sometimes attended from elsewhere. None the less, it was always a great relief to return home and resume our normal day to day routines. The fact that Sam had a somewhat unpredictable four legged companion when I was away was a concern but when, after some months, I found Gypsybella was sleeping curled up beside him, I knew the vet's advice had been good for us all.

CHAPTER ELEVEN

Surviving winter ice

The Albertan winters were longer and colder than anything I had previously experienced. I was concerned at how Sam would cope because we had seen much rain but little snow on our previous island home. Rain did not trouble him as ours had been rain forest country, and for a large part of each year I had worn fisherman's boots to walk to school. But the Alberta climate east of the Rockies was completely different. My first heavy snowfall occurred on the evening drive back from school when we were hit by a complete white out and the bus spun out of control off the road. No one was hurt and I recall that my main thoughts were for Sam. Shock has erased the immediate memories of the event itself.

By now Sam had the full run of a large piece of land surrounded by a high wooden fence behind the house but no day time shelter while I was at school. When I got home eventually after the accident, Sam was my first thought but there was no sign of him. Anxiously I scanned the garden area and to my relief I saw a black patch that proved to be his nose. He had dug a hole in the deep snow cover and made himself a cosy den, and after that I had no concern for his wellbeing. Gypsybella never went out in the snow and over the years proved to be a real house cat.

The railway line where we enjoyed our daily walks was little affected by ice and snow. The engines were equipped with snow ploughs and although the freight trains were infrequent, the rails seemed to remain clear. Snow did not build up on the embankment where the line was laid but lay deep on either side as Sam soon discovered when he plunged up to his neck in it. He and I were more interested in the tracks left by wildlife. I could tell when he put his nose to the ground that something was there. Bird tracks were common although I had yet to recognise them. There were small rodent tracks too, the distinctive line of their trailing tail clear in the snow. Occasionally they had come to a swift end, a flurry and a red patch showing where a bird had found or been found as a meal. We saw snowy owls very frequently perched in the trees nearest to the railway line.

My home in Alberta

The houses thinned out at my end of town and there was a small dug out lake between my home and the railway track. The earth from the excavation was piled into two long mounds, reminiscent to me of England's prehistoric long barrows. They seemed rather barren features although on a few occasions Sam had the excitement of chasing muskrats nearby. He enjoyed the water but when it froze over during our first Albertan winter it nearly cost him his life. I had noticed before the first snowfall that someone had constructed what I thought was a raft pulled up on the water's edge and I thought that it belonged to some local children although I never saw any on our walks. Indeed, on these outings, I seldom met anyone then or in subsequent years. People just did not walk, with or without dogs. When the lake and the much larger lake near to the school froze over I learnt that many of the staff were looking forward to skating. I was intrigued to hear people talk about ice augers and the need to test for an acceptable thickness before children and adults could put on their skates and venture out safely on to the ice. In this new life, I felt ready to try every fresh experience. I had never skated on ice and I found keeping my balance on any slippery surface difficult. The hazards of the school playground every winter was a tremendous challenge I could not avoid.

One day Sam ran out on to the frozen lake and plunged through a patch of thin ice. I had not yet heard of ice fishing where a hole is sawn through the ice and the angler sits on a box or stool on some form of platform with a baited line through the hole. I learnt later than this activity, simple in itself, can be quite elaborate and even comfortable with a shelter over the hole and hot drink facilities laid on, but this frozen over ice hole was the work of a real amateur. There was no indication to suggest thin ice and the 'raft' I had seen previously was some metres away from where Sam was now struggling to get out of the icy water. He was a very strong swimmer but all he could do was thrash around, desperately trying to get a grip on the surrounding ice. I watched and called encouragingly to him, my own fear mounting as I dare not risk going onto the ice myself. I knew that only a few minutes in such icy water can prove fatal. Then I thought of the 'raft'. "I'll be back," I called, a phrase I have used with all my dogs when leaving them for any reason, a day's work or in this case, as short a time as humanly possible as I was desperately scared. I knew the chances were that the wood would be frozen to the ground and I would not be able to move it but miraculously it came away with a violent tug.

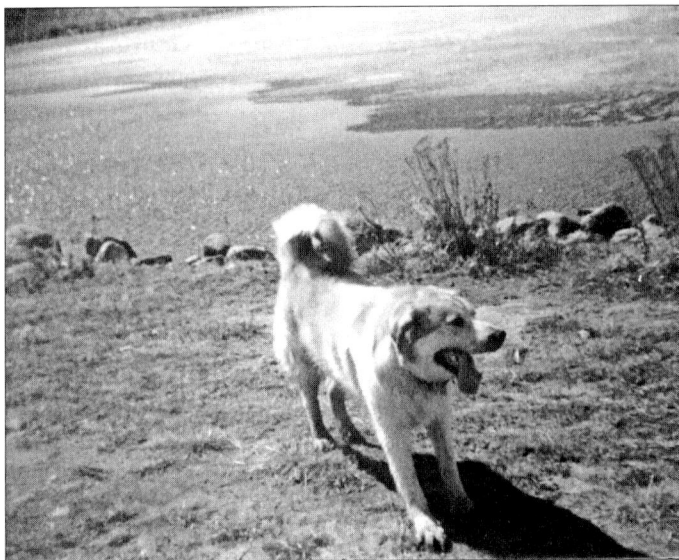

Sam and icy conditions, Alberta

I always carried a length of rope when out walking with Sam. I had found it on the Pacific shore after some past storm. Looped through Sam's collar it gave him more freedom to explore than a lead. I had been warned about the risk of meeting skunks or porcupines in Alberta, the former because it is so difficult cleaning an animal that has been sprayed and the latter because of its deadly quills. Fortunately we had never met either on our walks although I had smelled the result of a skunk's visit to someone's garden and occasionally, we saw dead porcupines on the road to school. Now, I pulled the rope through a gap in the frame and tugged it back to Sam, pushing it onto the ice as close as I could so that I could lie at full length in the hope of reaching him. Somehow I got the rope through his collar. By this time he had almost ceased struggling to get up onto the ice but the pull on his neck and the proximity of the platform and myself was sufficient for him to fight once more and heave himself out as I tugged. I do not recall much of the journey home. The whole event had been very traumatic. I was terrified that Sam could have been in the water too long and I was shivering uncontrollably with cold despite the feather filled padded coat I wore. I wrapped him up in a blanket and got into a bath of hot water myself. I was mightily relieved to find he was all right and unscathed next day. I was fine too, just rather shaken by what might have been a very different outcome.

The ice-hole experience did affect our walks for I no longer allowed him to run free until we reached the railway line and I began to explore some of the roads and tracks that crossed the line from east to west. The land had been divided on a grid system by the early settlers and any variation in the scenery was due more to nature than human intervention. As the seasons changed, I gradually changed the time of our walks, too, particularly as my work left me too tired to take Sam out after school. It was very peaceful to be out while the settlement was still asleep. One day I witnessed something that I might otherwise not have seen, the early morning removal of an entire house on a wide transporter. It had been jacked up and lifted in its entirety from the concrete walled basement to the vehicle prior to its journey to a new site. I would later see buildings on the move complete with police escort, often travelling long distances on the highways, but this North American scene was new to me at the time. What Sam made of the flashing lights and general activity I cannot imagine, but unlike most dogs he never barked and just stood watching silently at my side. I went back several times to see if another home was rising from the roofless basement rooms but the growth of vegetation was the only change I could detect, gradually obscuring the truncated pipes and electric wiring left in situ.

During this Albertan phase of my life in Canada, I saw much of my niece Carol and her growing family who lived to the south of Morinville. I experienced the welcome of Canadian style family Christmases, glitzy shopping malls and, after an evening visit, long drives home with ice chains on the tyres as we travelled on top of deep packed snow. Both my daughters came to Morinville at different times: Claudia Ruth visited one summer so we travelled around and Heather came out one Easter and spent time in my classroom. My older children, Claudia Ruth and Jeremy, had homes and work and their own children were growing up fast. I recognised that every school year proved harder than the last during term time and I realised why so many Canadian teachers seemed to prefer rented accommodation to owning their own house. Again, I saw much change over the years for, however idealistic some teachers were when they started teaching, the continuous pressure on our personal leisure time, the changes and extra-curricular activities in the evenings and even at the weekends became too great.

Despite the welcome holidays and time spent with my family – both Canadian relatives who had welcomed me so warmly into the extended clan and my grown up children and fast-growing grandchildren back in Europe – my health was slowly deteriorating again. By the end of my fifth winter in Alberta, my thoughts were frequently on retirement. I even began to think seriously about returning to the United Kingdom and what it would involve for Sam and Gypsybella. Finding information was harder in pre-internet days but with help, I obtained details for quarantine on entering the UK and the long term kennelling that would be required, a daunting consideration for both animals but particularly worrying in relation to Sam. It was hard to imagine such an enormous loving animal living alone within an enclosure for many months. Then there were transport requirements from Canada Air and costs involved, and of course a move would involve selling my house. By the time I had researched all the necessary details yet another teaching year had commenced and again I was fully committed to a new group of students.

CHAPTER TWELVE

Returning to Vancouver Island

Life is full of the unexpected! The first weeks of the next autumn term proved too much and my doctor said I must stop teaching immediately. I and my colleagues were all covered by a private health insurance negotiated when we joined the school and so there was no financial obstacle to accepting this advice. With much relief, at last I was able to put the responsibilities of a long and varied working life behind me and take the enforced period of rest required. That would enable me to regain my health and think about what might come next.

Over the years, several friends had accepted new teaching positions on Vancouver Island, British Columbia. It did not seem such an unfamiliar step to take as I had travelled on the island some years earlier. A cousin who lived there suggested that when my health was restored I moved there, staying with her until I could obtain another house. I had ample time now to plan, sift through the advice and suggestions that flooded in, and view the future with more optimism, something that had become sadly lacking in recent months.

The move when it came went smoothly thanks to all the help that came flooding in. Relocating would inevitably affect my contact with relatives too, on either side of the

91

Rockies. With my niece and her husband dealing with the sale of the house in Alberta and a cousin anxious to find another suitable property for me on Vancouver Island my main concern was the safe transit of Sam and my cat. Having previously found that Sam would need the largest cage supplied by the airline this was ordered. It came in three pieces, top, bottom and door but was easy to put together, a formidable hamper with padlock and key for extra security. Two memories stand out from that eventful flight from Edmonton. One, the awful moment at the airport when I watched my precious dog in his huge cage and Gypsybella's small cat hamper disappearing into the distance, knowing that they would be cooped up alone not understanding what was happening to them for a considerable time. I would not be able to see them when we arrived at Vancouver and I just had to rely on airport staff for their safe transfer to the smaller plane to Victoria.

The second memory is of our actual arrival. It turned out to be the funniest baggage collection I have ever experienced. My cousin met me as planned. Victoria airport seemed rather unsophisticated and small so she was able to park close to the building and meet me in the baggage room. This had one conveyer belt leading from outside through the conventional curtain, around the room and out again. The continuous slow motion was ideal for boxes, packages and cases, and we retrieved mine and waited patiently for Sam and Gypsybella to appear. There was quite a delay and by the time they came into view we were the only people still there. The cat was mewing piteously but Sam was standing looking through the grill of his great hamper, possibly as excited and relieved as I was to see them. Unfortunately we could not possibly retrieve him and in our consternation we missed grabbing the cat hamper too. Standing helplessly, we watched both animals exit through the curtain again, appearing and disappearing several times without anyone outside apparently noticing.

Frustration mixed with my delight at seeing them safe and sound. Concern ebbed away and I could see the funny side. In the end my cousin went off to find someone who could assist us and finally reappeared with a member of staff with a trolley. The conveyor belt was stopped and at last I could retrieve my pets. The trolley man was so intrigued by the whole situation that he not only conveyed our possessions to the car but helped undo the nuts and bolts that held Sam's cage together, the only way the car could accommodate everything. Meanwhile Sam had been able to stretch his legs around the parking lot and was ready to accompany us on the next stage of our journey. What he thought of the strangest day in his life who can tell?

At that time my cousin owned a property only a short drive from the small town where I planned to buy a house. Staying with her was enjoyable as we were both free to spend a few leisurely weeks visiting friends and exploring the forested regions at the lower end of Vancouver Island. One day we drove to a lovely stretch of the south west coast with Sam, walking along the deserted shore before we found a place for our picnic lunch. Sam raced in and out of the sea but showed no desire to take a long swim as he had done in the past, frequently returning to our side to share the joys of his life with us. We chose to stop at a waist high log, part buried in the sand, with a metre wide surface on which to sit, unpack our picnic and enjoy the endless view out over the Pacific Ocean. A remnant of some forest giant, already trimmed to a standard length and ready for the sawmill, it had obviously escaped some vast raft of timber and been washed ashore in a storm. It seemed a perfect spot to eat, talk, and enjoy the sun.

Relaxing after lunch and lazily looking towards the horizon, my cousin suddenly shouted, "Quick, we must get out of here. I'm sure that's a huge wave." All I could see was a long grey line where sky and sea met but the urgency in her voice was unmistakable. We swept our things into our bags, called to Sam who was near the water's edge, and raced for the steep bank leading to higher ground. Most people know about tsunamis now thanks to mass media, but at that time, despite my interest in geological matters, I had given the subject very little thought and did not know about the historic records relating to Vancouver Island and British Columbia's west coast. I heard the panic in my cousin's voice as we scrambled up to higher ground, helping each other and calling Sam who I knew would be close behind us. In fact he found an easier path and we reached the top together from different directions before daring to stop to look back.

Already our great log was tumbling around in a deeply troubled and churning sea. What had seemed to be its final resting place was gone and it would soon continue its journey to some other unknown shore. We had reached safety only just in time. My cousin said that there must have been some underwater seismic occurrence far out to sea to cause such a freak wave. I think she was more shaken with the experience than me. She realised how close to disaster our picnic outing had been. As in previous situations that had become dangerous, my only thought had been for my dog's safety. During the rest of my stay, we experienced a small earthquake that shook the chairs we were using but I knew that earth tremors were quite frequent and few people gave them much thought. Over subsequent years I had to straighten a few pictures that hung at odd angles. My brother showed me the safest place in my house should there be a big quake but it is easy to put such things to the back of one's mind. I learned to store water in case of sudden broken pipes and keeping tinned food supplies in case of mishap had been known since a wartime childhood. Being prepared was better than being over-anxious.

My cousin, Sam and I had a delightful time while I awaited the move into the house I had chosen on the outskirts of the small town of Duncan further north. We visited a number of smaller islands by ferry, walking for miles along the many winding country lanes so very reminiscent of the English countryside. It was not surprising that there were so many descendents of British Canadians settled in this part of Canada.

There comes a time, however, when the pleasures of recalling shared childhood and teenage memories are exhausted and it was a relief when the day eventually came for the animals and I to move on into our own space. The change probably meant little to Gypsybella as she had remained an indoor cat of her own choice. There were plenty of opportunities to explore but she preferred to sit and observe what went on around her, and our new home in Duncan had a sun deck which was ideal for her. I had arranged for the garden to be divided into two by a fence, the one adjacent to the house forming a secure enclosure for Sam. It contained a large gnarled plum tree and an old grape vine, and the sundeck provided shelter. A friend would later design and construct a large kennel, almost a small shed for him under one side of the deck where he could lie, but for many months he had easy access to a very large basement consisting of the furnace room for my oil fired central heating and two very large rooms. A staircase led to the four upstairs rooms and Sam used to mount them three steps at a time, descending the same way. I think he enjoyed our latest home as much as I did.

Daily walks with Sam first consisted of getting to know the small town of Duncan before we ventured further afield. As with my previous experience in Alberta, we did not encounter other dog walkers but it was an ideal way to make new friends and acquaintances. Unlike many Canadian settlements, it also had a distrinctive historical central area of red brick and wooden buildings that was easy to explore on foot. I found, too, that Sam was welcomed in a number of places including the bank, the flower shop, the second-hand furniture store where I became a good customer as I gradually added items to our home, and the book shop. The latter, which we visited frequently, was unforgettable. Floor to ceiling bookcases divided a relatively small space into a series of dimly lit corridors, each too narrow for Sam to turn so that he had to back out of some of them. Wherever there was a corner leading to the next rows of shelves, it was likely to find the elderly owner, perched on a stool. He was always pleased to see us, and did not seem to expect to make a sale although I am sure he was glad when one took place. He just loved books and welcomed any visitor, and his benevolence was extended to Sam who received an occasional pat on the head when the old man was not holding some ancient volume.

We lived very close to the edge of Duncan and I soon found an area where Sam could enjoy complete freedom. It was a flat area of what must have been farmland which lay between the Canada Highway, the road that ran north-south along the length of Vancouver Island, and a less used road leading off to the west. This abandoned patch of land retained a group of very old apple trees where I was able to harvest windfalls every autumn but there was no sign of the original farmstead. The old wooden buildings which were either raised off the ground or had dirt floors had left no visible trace although I always hoped to find some clue to who might have once lived there. Sam and I enjoyed the area almost daily, and I even sat and sketched there from time to time, enjoying the sense of solitude, while he explored the scrub around me. No one ever warned me to keep an eye alert for bears during the fruit season or indeed for cougars. Perhaps they thought, if it even crossed their minds, that I knew about such hazards. I regarded our tranquil setting as a relic fragment of English countryside recognisable from childhood. The roads on Vancouver Island were a different matter. I found it very stressful to walk even a short distance at the side of the Highway to reach open land on the far side, and, although Sam and I explored the area to the west, it was more out of a wish to find what was there than for the enjoyment of a different walk.

We had the old farm site to ourselves for several years, only meeting one person, a woman who lived in her small vehicle and parked there for a few days. I was just beginning to get to know her when one morning I found she had gone and we never saw her again. Then without warning, a construction team moved in and I sadly watched my apple trees torn up and the walks we had loved turn to ugly scars where the greenery had been stripped away. It was the beginning of a new bypass to connect the highway and our local road and signalled the eventual end of our 'country' walks.

CHAPTER THIRTEEN

A change of pace

We had been living in Duncan for about two years when Sam's annual health check revealed that he had a lump which the vet said needed removing as soon as possible. It was an utter shock as I was so used to his sturdy presence and companionship that I had seldom thought about his age. My retirement years were proving interesting, enjoyable and very busy. I was facilitating two Spanish classes, teaching English as a foreign language, running several adult education courses at the local college and doing a range of other voluntary tasks that included working in local politics. I joined two clubs for expatriates and an outdoor activities group who explored the coast nearby and local islands using an old privately owned cruiser. We met at Cowichan Bay and our trips tooks us considerable distances, sometimes to islands under American control where our skipper seemed to have little need of paperwork for the time we spent ashore. Away from these sea trips across an international boundary marked more rigidly on paper than on water, I also joined a local walking group. Sam could accompany me on these hikes through former logged territory or along the cleared strips of land where electricity pylons stretched for miles through otherwise inaccessible forested areas. In addition we always had our daily walks.

I made frequent visits to the local First Nations tourist attraction and cultural heritage centre where occasionally I ran into old acquaintances from my early years on the west coast further north. Sometimes they remembered and enquired after Sam and were astonished that he was still alive and well. On the day of Sam's operation it seemed the only place where I might find comfort and support. In the centre of the large traditionally designed wooden hall displaying a variety of locally produced carvings, knitted outdoor wear and the occasional stone sculpture (from elsewhere), there was a large chest draped with a magnificent wolf skin. It was not for sale and I was never quite sure why it was there, but I was drawn to it and often stroked the thick coat as I passed. I now found solace in its presence, recalling the times when Sam was young, and my own years spent teaching and living so closely with people who honoured their own affinities to Raven, Killer Whale and the Wolf Clan. Seeking strength, I prayed to their Great Spirit for a safe outcome to his operation. I am not sure how long I stayed there or how I spent the long afternoon that followed, but how I welcomed the vet's phone call to say that Sam was all right.

I had to accept once Sam was safely home again that he was beginning to show his age. He no longer took the basement steps in two or three great leaps and sometimes chose to remain in the garden or downstairs rather than spending the evening with Gypsybella and me. Otherwise the daily pattern of our lives continued happily and the tumour did not reappear.

One amusing incident during my time in Duncan was the annual visit of a travelling circus. It was still considered acceptable to many people for performances by dogs, horses, lions and elephants to take place, and the majority of circus folk who visited the town ensured the wellbeing of their animals. From previous visits I knew that the elephants were outside quite early each morning on a patch of ground where Sam and I often walked following the loss of our farm land to construction. We had met the elephants before and Sam just accepted their presence. On this occasion I stopped for a brief chat with their keeper as there were rumours that it might be the circus's last visit due to protests having been made about their use of animals. He was extremely worried because it was his livelihood at stake and the wellbeing of all the circus families. My thoughts were on what he was saying and not the close proximity of the nearer elephant to Sam. The former suddenly decided to empty its bladder, the reason it was out there and Sam was in full range. I had never appreciated until that moment how much liquid an elephant can eject so suddenly. Despite moving quickly I got sprayed and Sam much to his surprise received a lot more. The keeper was apologetic but very amused. Poor man, he had little to smile about that season, and it was the last time the circus came to Duncan.

Over the next two years Sam and I spent more time in the garden rather than exploring the local countryside. He still enjoyed our daily walks but at a slower pace and, as there were bear traps located in several strategic places including one very close to home, I began to consider our safety for the first time. During the apple season bears were attracted to the trees on outlying properties and, having heard of someone losing their small dog to some unfortunate encounter, I became alert to this possible danger which was probably general knowledge to most longterm island residents. Occasionally bears ventured into town and one was seen in my own road, probably the reason for the sudden appearance of a bear cage in the parking area of the local library. When trapped, the bears were conveyed to a safe distance from town before being released.

Sam, Vancouver Island

Sam was much beloved by one of my next door neighbours, an elderly lady who liked to talk with me when I was gardening. When Sam started accompanying me into the cultivated part of our garden he would go to the low fence where it was easy for the lady to stroke his head and talk to us both. She and her husband both enjoyed this friendship with Sam. My neighbours on the other side were afraid of Sam because of his size. What they thought of his wolf howl I never knew. He raised his nose to the sky and howled very seldom, but his friends next door loved to hear him and always commented on it when we next met. I wondered whether he was communicating with some distant call from the mountains which we could not hear.

When Sam began to avoid the basement steps instead of plodding up them to sleep in the kitchen at night, I knew the signs and moved his bedding down to the furnace room. He was quite happy to curl up in the warmth, but continued to use his outdoor shelter under the sundeck during the day even in the winter. He liked the space outside where he could see and hear what was going on. He had to navigate the three steps from the furnace room to garden level but seemed to accept the stiffness in his legs and other limitations.

One morning I found he could not get up. He was too heavy to lift and I could see from his eyes that he had quietly reached the end of the wonderful life we had so enjoyed together. He was a little over fourteen and a half. The vet and his assistant could not have been more kind, leaving me to grieve alone but telling me to ring the practice if I needed someone.

I only fully appreciated the vet's professional friendship and consideration a short time later when Gypsybella died suddenly. She was walking across the room one evening to settle in her usual place on the settee when she had what the vet later called, a heart attack. I called the emergency line and he arrived in a matter of minutes but it was too late. Completely baffled he asked if he could do an autopsy as she had showed no sign of anything being wrong. She had searched the entire house after Sam's death and I am sure missed him. It turned out that she had had a congenital heart condition never picked up by the three vets who had handled her, but it explained a lot. Apart from her initial meeting with Sam in Alberta when she had scratched his nose, she was the quietest cat I have ever had who had never ventured into a garden and preferred bird watching from the sundeck to attempting to stalk and catch one. With the loss of these two companions who had been such constants of my life in Canada, and no family living close, I was now very alone!

That veterinary practice remains in my memory as a model of what all such practices should be. At the loss of a pet everyone at the surgery put their names on a card of condolence, a small kindly gesture but how much it helped. What a different attitude this is to a request for immediate payment while the owner of some precious companion is still in a state of grief and shock.

CHAPTER FOURTEEN

Rescued just in time

The chasm left by losing Sam and Gypsybella was immense. Sam had been both companion and friend while Gypsybella had offered comfort with her indoor presence. I had no desire to replace either of them and spent ever more time on my hobbies and volunteer work. It seemed to be the most effective way of relieving depression and loneliness. Days and routines organised around animal care since I had first come to Canada required filling differently. An empty house was hard to come back to. Looking back on that period I think I was managing reasonably well but at least one friend had different thoughts on the subject. She lived on her own a little way out of town and often dropped in, in typical Canadian style, for a cup of tea and a cookie when passing by.

One day she arrived full of concern: there had been a dog round up on the First Nation lands in the vicinity of her home. The dogs were being held at a local kennels for a very short period prior to being put down unless homes could be found for them. She did not know that I had experienced culling of dogs previously in Alberta and British Columbia and my own views on the problems caused by having unneutered dogs freely breeding in a community already beset by many human tragedies. My friend felt I might be interested in acquiring another dog and saving a canine life. I was not yet mentally or emotionally ready for this step but her persuasion and the scenes I had previously witnessed prompted me to accompany her to the dog pound.

I barely remember those dogs. They were a dispirited and cowed bunch of small indeterminate mixed breeds, accustomed to surviving outside by their own wiliness and not used to being deprived of freedom. They stood behind a wire fence and were wary of human contact. Only one approached where we stood, a little black and white creature who seemed fearless and friendly. She seemed too young to have experienced human unkindness and living by her wits, and the thought of what lay ahead for her was too sad to contemplate. As my friend had anticipated, I found almost by accident that I had acquired another dog.

She came with a name, Abu, probably given to her by a group of children who had treated her as an adorable toy until she outgrew that role and they had abandoned her to fend for herself. I was not happy with the name as I felt it might have some meaning of which I was not aware but, before I had found an alternative, I introduced her to the group of ladies who met once a week in my house to learn Spanish. Abu had quickly made herself at home, sensing the renewed security which she had experienced so briefly in her short life. She was friendly and playful, and had a funny habit of suddenly chasing her own tail which made visitors laugh. It seemed appropriate that 'risa', the Spanish word for laugh or laughter, should be added to her name and so she became Aburisa from then on.

Unfortunately only two days later when the male equivalent of my ladies' Spanish class took place, another side to Aburisa's character was revealed. Without warning she launched herself at the ankles of one of the men who was meeting her for the first time. The attack was so aggressive that only the quick action of another class member prevented him from being bitten. He lived in the area where she had been rounded up but said he had never seen her on or close to his land. He also liked dogs. Perhaps there was some odour she had detected that had engendered fear and her unwarranted attack but from then on I was wary of her behaviour when I introduced her to any stranger. The immediate result was that she lost the freedom of the house when there were visitors, a sad beginning to our relationship, but the risk was too great to do otherwise.

Aburisa seemed at ease in the presence of all women, and was friendly to most men including my elder brother who visited me from the mainland once a month. She liked my neighbours, too, so perhaps she felt more secure in the presence of the elderly although the person she had attacked without any provocation on his part was not a young man. However, I kept her on a very short leash when we went out, and this coupled with the knowledge of bears in the vicinity meant walks became a duty rather than a pleasure. I was able to appreciate her small size as she could fit into my friends' cars and accompany me to their more distant homes. Sam had always been welcome when I visited friends on foot but despite being loved by all, drivers felt uncomfortable with a dog bigger than themselves occupying a seat close to them.

Aburisa was at her best in my garden. Initially I thought she might dig her way to freedom under the solid high wooden fence but from the moment she saw the old plum tree it became her special domain. I had never owned a dog who climbed trees and when she first jumped up and walked along the lowest branch I feared she might attempt to escape via the sundeck. I immediately took precautions, lining the nearest side with hardboard, but I do not think she ever considered walking to the end of the nearest branch. She liked climbing, jumping from one branch to another until she reached the place of her choice where she would stand and view the neighbourhood for long periods of time. Occasionally she would lie down, but I used to think that she felt safer standing, perhaps alert to imagined perils she might have encountered in the past.

Aburisa, Duncan, c.1998

Strangely I have limited memories of the few years that I cared for this little dog. I do not think we established any real bond despite the companionship of having an animal living in the house. Her well-being, happiness and safety was important, but she seemed as happy in the kennels I had used for years when I went away for a holiday as she did on my return. I cannot recall any excited greeting when I came home, but my memory could be at fault here. Less remote than in either of my previous Canadian homes, it was easier for more relatives to visit me in Duncan. Nieces and nephews, and their own children, came by and and I had the pleasure of watching another generation exploring opportunities. It was a comfort as my children, and four grandchildren already, were growing up, far away in London and Spain, although I have very happy memories of lovely holidays when my son and two daughters each visited at different times. So did a grand daughter who came with a friend and we all went for a flight with one of my nephews as pilot. No one had followed me permanently to Canada as I had hoped, even though, in my remote float house years before, I'd even furnished a room in the hope that they would come and stay.

It was a time when I lost a number of friends. Many were ex-pats who had moved to Canada in the early 1950s and were considerably older than myself, but each loss, particularly within the groups of regular visitors, was sad and unsettling, something we all experience as we age. The greatest loss of all was that of my elder brother. We had developed a deep friendship which had somewhat made up for the many years we had been separated in the earlier part of our lives. A strong motivation in my returning to Canada in 1980 was a deep desire to get to know my brothers better and, although the time I had been granted with the younger of the two had been prematurely cut short, I had been blessed with the love and friendship of my older sibling and the times we had together.

In the spring of 2000, shortly before I joined my youngest daughter and husband for a holiday, I had been approached by the real estate agent who had originally dealt with my purchase of the house. At his suggestion, it was arranged that in my absence he should hold an open day to gauge the value and interest in the property should I ever decide to move. With Aburisa safely in kennels I went away and thought little more about it, knowing I could trust him. I was curious about how much my home had appreciated in value during my time of living in Duncan. The valuation and, after my return from holiday, an even more advantageous offer, led to a rapid chain of events that I had never imagined. During the preceding twenty years, and particularly, since the loss of Sam and Gypsybella, I must admit I had weighed up the pros and cons of returning to the United Kingdom where my youngest daughter and husband still lived. It was a hastily made decision, with all the consequences of such a relocation for my Canadian friends and relatives.

Once focused on returning to England, Aburisa was my only real problem. I never considered taking her with me to face the months of expensive quarantine that such an action would have necessitated. The only criticism I ever received for leaving the little dog was from her new owner, a friend of a friend, who knew nothing of her background or mine and took her on at face value. With more freedom than I had ever been able to provide and as an owner with a large property and a car, I sensed that Aburisa would have a happy and relatively long life ahead of her. My years in Canada were over.

CHAPTER FIFTEEN

Walking English country lanes again

In the summer of 2000, I found myself moving into a new home, this time in Yorkshire. Yet again all my things travelled through the Panama Ship Canal and across the Atlantic. With a beautiful view of the hills and dales on the edge of the Peak National park, my new little house was within walking distance of my daughter, Heather, and her husband's property and my latest granddaughter. All I needed was a dog, for now I knew I was at last mentally ready to welcome a four legged companion who I hoped would become a friend.

We found her at a local RSPA rescue centre and I knew from the moment I saw her she would be both lovable and loving. There was collie, perhaps Sheltie, in her genes. Ginger brown and white in colour, she was a medium sized dog with a lovely silky plume of a tail which she carried proudly, and soft tufted ears and a ruff of hair framing her face. She needed a lot of grooming but she still left long silky hairs around the house, a small price to pay for her affectionate presence. She had been estimated at fifteen weeks old when abandoned in the heart of Halifax, left tied to a bollard in the middle of a road. Micro chips were still in their infancy at the beginning of the new millennium so her owners were untraceable. Her terrifying experience gave her a lasting fear of heavy traffic, particularly motor bikes. Fortunately she enjoyed travelling by car and always responded to an outing with pleasure. Within weeks of my arrival, and after being approved as a suitable owner, we took her home at the height of the blackberry season. I named her Bramble.

Those early months are a bit of a blur now as I was busy with unpacking and trying to fit the contents of a much larger Canadian home into an English semi-detached house. There was the difference in culture, too, as I was now an 'incomer' viewed with suspicion. In Canada I had become accustomed to getting to know strangers over a cup of coffee, and it would take several years before I fully accepted that people in Yorkshire still did not drop in to have a cuppa in order to get acquainted.

My daily walks with Bramble, however, soon provided a very diverse number of acquaintances as we explored the neighbourhood. Dog walkers were willing to say hello. We kept to the roads at first as I had been away too long to lose an instinctive fear of something lurking behind the trees or drystone walls. Soon we began to explore bridle tracks and pathways up onto the surrounding moorland. There were other walkers enjoying the scenery as they exercised their dogs, and even when they were lost in thought or enjoying their own company, their dogs had a different approach. Immediately alert to any other four legged stranger in the vicinity they knew whether it was a friend or foe.

Bramble soon made two very different friends as their walks coincided with ours. One was a Jack Russell and the other an Irish Wolf hound, and while the dogs communicated we owners talked and I began to learn about the locality. There would be many more dogs over the years who came and went but I think these first friends were the most important in Bramble's life, helping her to establish her place in the local canine society. She enjoyed going out but I had to hold her close and reassure her when I heard the distant sound of an approaching motorbike. The only other hazard was the milk tanker that still made daily collections from the few remaining local dairy farms. Its timing varied but the size, bulk and engine frightened Bramble to such an extent that I would scan the hillsides daily to see where it was parked, whether it looked stationary or the direction it was taking. I could see for miles from our upland walks and over time, if the tanker unexpectedly approached us from behind, I gained local knowledge of where the nearest four-barred field gate might be found. They provided a deeper and safer recess for her than the narrow verges and high dry stone walls that bordered most of our local roads around my new Yorkshire home.

Bramble – 2001

Bramble seemed to like the dairy cattle in the local fields and over several summers she established an acquaintance through the bars of one gate with two cows. They approached out of curiosity at first, but the daily nose to nose encounters seemed to have some significance, and Bramble always appeared puzzled when she found the field empty due to a temporary change of grazing. She was unfazed by the movement of sheep or even a runaway horse we once encountered, but we were both unprepared for a car-load of dogs.

We were returning from a tranquil walk on the moor. The track led directly to where our lane made an abrupt right-angled turn close to a patch of waste ground where cars occasionally parked. I had barely noticed the approach of a small car until it stopped and the owner got out. Opening both side and rear doors the woman released at least five dogs who headed straight for us and the track. They seemed to be dogs of all sizes and I was never certain whether there were some little ones between the whirl of legs and excited barks and yaps that suddenly filled the silence. My immediate reaction was to freeze, past memories of being knocked down by a pack of feral dogs attacking Sam flooding my thoughts. I had already put Bramble back on her lead before we approached the road and I found she was cowering beside me. When I recovered my wits, I realized the dogs had passed us by, intent on their temporary freedom. That sudden encounter shocked me: I had not come across paid dogwalkers taking out numerous dogs before. Perhaps it had emerged during my years in Canada? From then on, the occasional sight of anything resembling that little car and its possible occupants made me change our route for the day. I saw the dogs several times that year from a safe distance before their routine changed or they moved away.

Bramble shared many family outings, enjoying the thrill of new places, sniffing out new smells, or trying to chase squirrels and birds just for the fun of making them run or fly away. My daughter took her for many walks, too, enjoying the exercise and some relaxation. Bramble just enjoyed life, and spent as much time in my garden as I did, exploring and returning to see what I was doing from time to time. During holiday times, we would enjoy house-visiting too: she and I would spend time on a property that became home from home and she soon learnt how far she could safely explore before returning to my side.

Bramble had a loving, friendly and gentle personality so that she just accepted the somewhat unpredictable behaviour of my latest two small grandchildren, retiring to her basket in the corner of the dining room when they visited. As they got older she submitted to being led around the house as if she was a toy, accompanied by one or two of their own toy dogs on make shift leads. She never protested, but I finally had to put a stop to this. Later on, they would take turns preparing her food while she used to stand on her hind legs and bouncing in a series of little jumps while her bowl was filled. It was an endearing habit and a daily mealtime ritual that never failed to bring delight.

Bramble had the same gentle approach to my daughter's cat, Pushkin. For some considerable time when we were visiting, Pushkin viewed Bramble from the safety of their staircase but I was delighted when cat and dog finally met at floor level. When I saw him rub his head against Bramble's neck, I knew that he had at last accepted her as part of his family.

Bramble had very keen hearing and heard the slightest unusual sound outside our own home, alerting me to the approach of strangers which I found invaluable. Where some dogs react with growls or a frenzied barking she stood or sat listening intently, with her head a little to one side, indicating the direction from which the noise had come. Unfortunately for her, this sensitivity had an adverse effect as each firework season approached. Having lived for so many years overseas where fireworks were only used in mass displays to celebrate a special occasion, I had forgotten the indiscriminate way fireworks are often used in the United Kingdom. A fireworks company was based not far from my new home providing jobs and perhaps even discounted sales. This ready supply may explain why loud bangs and whistles occurred not only days before the 5th November but for some time later.

With their ever growing power and noise, the explosions seem devised to give some people's hearts an unpleasant jolt. Fireworks terrify many animals and Bramble was no exception. Whether it was something that whirled and whistled around the walls or rooftop, clattered like an anti-aircraft gun, or sounded powerful enough to make the windows cave in, there was no where she could hide. Turning up the volume of a radio or television never helped, and it was annually something she, like many dogs and other animals, have to suffer. Having watched the fear and disorientation of animals I love dearly, I fail to understand why there is no legislation to control the indiscriminate use of fireworks. I believe that firework use condones cruelty, and tranquilisers are not the answer when the random detonations and the resultant fear may become life-long.

Bramble loved toys. She was given several squeaky toys but they did not last long. I discouraged them as gifts when I discovered the squeak inside was just wrapped in a plastic bag and was dangerously small. She had always been intrigued at the area of the toy where the squeak was emitted and her attempts to locate it were often too successful for my peace of mind. Another favourite toy was a doorstop which closely resembled a rather loveable puppy and was often playfully purloined by the children. I often found it in her basket after their visits, but was never quite certain who had put it there as it was used for an upstairs door and was rather heavy to be dragged downstairs unseen or unheard. One popular toy was a solid many sided red ball with built in cavities which made it easy for her to grip. It was too big for any danger of swallowing but small enough to roll under furniture which kept Bramble busy for long periods as she investigated its position from all angles and tried to work out how to retrieve it. Her delight when it was returned to her was very enjoyable to watch.

Bramble's collection also included a solid rubber yellow bone. She took it to her basket at night and it was invariably close to her during the day except on the few occasions when she hid it and played with something else. I sometimes came across it, perhaps in a remote corner or under a cushion, the latter a place where one might not expect to find it as she preferred her basket to a chair and never played on the furniture. If left in place, she knew exactly where it was and would re-find it with great excitement as if she had made a new discovery. It was part of her many endearing qualities and made her so beloved by everyone who knew her.

It was Easter 2011, a time of year when Bramble and I had lovely long walks and also spent a lot of time on my daughter and family's property when they were away visiting friends in Italy. When I went downstairs one morning, instead of being greeted by the excitement of another new day I found Bramble lying quietly in her basket. I could not see anything wrong and she did not seem to have any pain anywhere. She just did not want to move. Of more concern was that she did not want anything to eat or drink. Without transport of my own and living some considerable distance from a vet I hesitated before telephoning them for advice, knowing that the morning was their busiest time. As I expected they could not arrange a visit until late afternoon, during which time I had sat on the floor beside Bramble comforting her and hoping she would show some improvement.

The vet came with an assistant and having made a cursory examination told me she was very weak which of course I knew. He then asked somewhat abruptly if I had a pet insurance to which I said 'no'. It so happened that for the first time in my life with dogs I had taken out an insurance in her early years, purely because it was a novelty to me and a cheap offer which I could afford. I had not come across pet insurances before. I had kept up the premiums for some years but had become disconcerted by the scale of the annual increase. When I questioned this I was told that with every year my pet was getting older and the likelihood of illness was greater. How true, but I had lived through a different era where a no-claim had been annually rewarded with a bonus. My dogs had always lived long and healthy lives, and I had finally discontinued the insurance. In the event I do not think in Bramble's case it would have made any difference except to my financial liability.

Not satisfied with the results of the examination the vet said that he needed an x-ray and more tests back at the surgery. They departed with my precious dog promising to telephone me as soon as possible. I cannot recall even having a moment to say goodbye. Certainly I had no idea I would not see her again. Poor little Bramble! When the call came I was told she had had a ruptured spleen, presumably a genetic weakness as nothing had occurred in her life to have caused it and they could not save her. The news was devastating. With my nearest family members away, I had no means of bringing her home for interment close to other family pets who had been buried in the wood she had so loved. I had the consolation of phone calls, particularly from my son, Jeremy, in Spain and also a call from Italy, but it was a particularly difficult time. I could not help comparing the sympathy I had received when Sam and Gypsybella had died in Canada to just receiving an invoice from the veterinary practice a few days later for the care I am sure they had given my much loved dog. Some days later I received a letter from an old school friend in the United States with whom I had shared my grief. She enclosed a memorial card which reads as follows:

"In loving memory of Jennie and Bramble who never met each other but were both so very much loved and best of companions and important parts of the lives of the Grange family of New Paltz, NY., and of Dorothy an old and dear school friend living in Yorkshire U.K. Jennie and Bramble, you will always be missed, and I know you will be Best Friends at Angels Rest the other side of the Rainbow Ridge." Angels Rest is a Memorial Garden.

Receiving this at that particular moment in time meant a lot to me and helped to fill the void Bramble had left.

CHAPTER SIXTEEN

Another faithful friend

With advancing years the idea of having another pet is perhaps foolish, but when living alone, the practicalities of such thoughts are not fully considered. On their return from holiday, my younger daughter and family had been as saddened by my loss of Bramble as other family members. I recall my granddaughters suggesting a variety of possible new companions for me ranging from a cat and a parrot to a Chihuahua. Knowing that the usual channels for rehoming a dog with an older person would be out of the question, they and their parents turned to the internet. Different charities were contacted and, in a very short time, Leo arrived.

Leo was brought by van from a considerable distance. He was an undernourished stray who we were told could not be housed by the nearest rescue centre as it was already full and he was being temporarily housed by another charity equally stretched for accommodation. The lady asked few questions, checked that the garden was well fenced, assured us that he was a good traveller, accepted a donation, and left the trembling dog in my care.

Leo, the name given on the health check and record book, had been substituted for another name, and the description had been altered to a cross breed, an untreated black whippet with white points. I did not look at it until after she had left, as there were things I should have questioned, but my thoughts were on the dog. He had the appearance of a small greyhound, but brought back memories of another black long-legged dog of a different breed some fifty years previously, also shivering with fear of the unknown, his large eyes imploringly seeking someone to trust and love and be loved in return. I knew immediately that Leo, like Sebastian of long ago, would need much love and reassurance in the years to come.

I was shocked to find that my new dog was not house trained. At first I put this down to nerves as he was a very frightened dog. Left briefly on his own Leo tried to escape through the bay window, almost emptying the bookcase in front of it in his attempt to reach the spacious window sill. I found the heavy volumes scattered on my return, fortunately undamaged. Another attempt to restrain him in the kitchen resulted in his pulling his head out of his collar, something I did not repeat. However, he regarded the entire kitchen floor as a cat might regard a litter tray, which was fortunate for the rest of the house, but just one of Leo's problems through no fault of his own.

A vet put my new companion's age at eight or more years. He thought Leo had been living by his wits for some considerable time and would soon be restored to health. He said that at some time there had been an injury to a front leg and pointed out that the dog had lost part of an ear. I soon found that contrary to what I had been told, he was not a good traveller and any journey by car made him sick. Tablets from the vet did not help and though we tried several times it did restrict any journey or outing by car with my grandchildren. Fortunately he walked well on a lead, and the only time he needed a strong arm was the odd occasions when a squirrel or cat crossed the road or when there was a sudden crack from a firework. It was far safer to miss our afternoon walk as the days around November 5th were a terrifying ordeal for him and difficult for me. He had very acute hearing and picked up the distant bangs well before I heard a crack, fizz or whine locally.

My knowledge of greyhounds was very limited and as with any new dog, new knowledge comes with every passing day. Gradually their different characters, intelligence levels and behaviour patterns are revealed, while at the same time affection, trust and understanding grow on both sides. My knowledge, depth of feeling and love were considerably enhanced when a leaking pipe and structural damage brought builders and a couple of mature cleaners into our home. The women took an immediate interest in my dog. Leo liked to know what was going on and silently watched from a safe distance, often around a corner where he could easily back out of sight. He seldom trusted people enough to approach them but accepted women more readily than men.

The cleaners wanted to know all about him. They noted his damaged ear and told me it was probably where a registration number had been torn off before he was abandoned so the owner could not be traced. The thought of Leo being mutilated in such a way was horrendous. I learnt that some people kept his breed in wire cages, often in kitchens, and used them just for racing or hare coursing to make money. Once they ceased to be winners they were discarded. I hoped such stories were exaggerated but a few months later a chance conversation with a regular delivery man confirmed what they had said. He, too, was interested when he first saw Leo and told me that his brother had two similar dogs, kept caged when not working. Some visits later he mentioned that his brother had won a substantial sum with the dogs. The next time I asked about the dogs he said that his brother had only one now as the other had proved useless. I never mentioned them again.

Leo had no interest in toys. He spent much of his time in the house sleeping and chose an old armchair for his bed with his head hanging down to the floor or resting over one arm with his long nose pointing to the ceiling, uncomfortable positions but he liked it that way. Whenever I left a room he followed me, standing quietly watching until my task was completed. It was the same in the garden: I think my enjoyment of gardening was a complete mystery to him and he refused to enter the greenhouse even when there was sudden rain. As he hated getting wet he had some fear perhaps of the limited space although he chose the nearby paved area as a permanent place to relieve himself. He never asked to go out when we were in the house so I had to establish a routine. This worked well. He liked routines and when he went into the garden on his own he always followed the same tracks that he had gradually formed through and around trees and shrubs in preference to the paths that I had established.

Many animals have remarkable memories including recognition of human communication through both sound and sign language. I recall when I was a child teaching our dogs commands in school girl French which they soon accepted as easily as English. We even tried German but this was frowned upon by the family and our experiment soon lost our interest. Dogs have the ability to pick out certain meaningful words in conversation which have been deliberately altered to mislead them. They appear to recognise complete phrases and will listen intently when someone talks to them when time is spent with just one person. In particular they remember individual names which perhaps they associate with a family member with whom they temporarily bonded on a visit. Leo knew the names of all my immediate family, and whenever I received overseas telephone calls I told him the name of the caller. Sometimes they spoke to him and he showed recognition of the voice with varying degrees of pleasure, though what he made of it can only be guessed. On their infrequent visits he just accepted their presence as if there had not been many months since he last saw them, although with children it took longer for full acceptance, perhaps because of the change in their size.

Leo's one and only visit to kennels took place about two years after he had joined me. I had to have a hip replacement and, although my time away from home would be brief, his occasional nocturnal visits to the kitchen made it impossible for him to stay with my daughter and her family as they had a dog of their own by now. It must have been yet another terrifying experience for him though he had the best possible care and understanding. My son, Jeremy, flew in from Spain to care for us both temporarily on my discharge from hospital. He had two Old English Sheep dogs of his own at the time and shared memories of most of my former four legged companions. Leo was familiar with his voice over the phone and was very happy to be back home with us both until I could cope safely on my own.

I found it became necessary to get help with cleaning but there seemed to be constant staffing problems – people not turning up due to illness or perhaps the non-arrival of a child minder. On one occasion, the young owner of the cleaning company asked her mother to cover for an absentee. The mother took an immediate interest in Leo. She had an elderly dog, too, and she offered to take Leo for daily walks with her own. At the time I imagine neither of us considered how long this arrangement would last. I thought of it as a temporary measure, as I still hoped to regain full mobility, but Leo had found new friends, a lady in whom he had complete trust and a small Heinz variety rescued dog with a similarly sad background. When they first met they seemed to establish an immediate bond. Tiny, so aptly named, reached less than halfway up Leo's long legs, and stood quietly while Leo checked him out and found the smells safe and satisfactory. Tiny was a complete contrast to Leo, with multi coloured long hair and an immediate trusting friendly nature. The two dogs liked each other, and Tiny accepted me from the moment we met on the back doorstep. It was an unexpected friendship that was to continue for years. The consideration for my well-being and that of my dog extended through three generations of the same family and they made sure that if one person was not available to take Leo for his walk some other member of the family collected Leo regardless of the very changeable Yorkshire weather. When Tiny succumbed to old age, Leo's daily outings continued, and I believe his presence in the moorland areas, enjoyed by both dogs for so long, also helped the dogwalkers' grief at the loss of their own little companion.

In due course another rescued dog joined the daily walk but Leo showed no interest in the new companion. The feeling was apparently mutual. The dogs seemed to ignore each other from their first meeting. I found this interesting as Leo had established a good relationship with a dog now owned by another member of the same family, and although they met very infrequently, Harley and he became good friends, showing pleasure each time they met.

Leo began to show his age some time before I had to face the inevitability of losing him. Several inexplicable illnesses occurred, variously treated, from which he rallied, recovered and was ready for his walks again. Sometimes he walked very slowly, and his walkers gave me frequent health reports, but at times he showed his old energy and was laughingly dubbed the dog with nine lives. Apart from his walks he liked to keep me within view, even when I went into the garden or up and down the stairs which I think he found difficult at times. He alone among all my dogs did not decide that the time had come to leave stairs to others, and one morning there was a sudden crash and I found him at the bottom, seemingly unconscious amid the debris of a table of cactii which he had knocked over. There was little a vet could do and a few days later just before Christmas 2019 we had to say goodbye. He was laid to rest close to other much loved pets in our family wood, the place where he had finally found peace and happiness in a very long life.

Leo would be the last of my wonderful lifetime companions. What love they have all given me and what joy and friendship they have shared. Their memories will live on.